MAN IN THE EVERGLADES

Copeland Studies in Florida History · No. 3

Published in cooperation with

THE EVERGLADES NATURAL HISTORY ASSN.

MAN
IN THE
EVERGLADES

*2000 Years of Human History
in the Everglades National Park*

CHARLTON W. TEBEAU

UNIVERSITY OF MIAMI PRESS *Coral Gables · Florida*

Second, revised edition 1968
(The first edition was published in 1964 under the title
THEY LIVED IN THE PARK:
The Story of Man in the Everglades National Park.)

Seventh printing 1986

To Leon and James Henry

CONTENTS

ILLUSTRATIONS

MAPS

Illustration Acknowledgments

National Park Service, pp. 20, 27, 35, 74, 120, 128, 158, 159, 163; T. R. Alexander, pp. 24, 25; F. C. Craighead, p. 28; Florida State Museum, pp. 39, 40; Courtesy Mrs. M. K. Ashworth, p. 51; *Tropic Magazine*, 1917, p. 54; *Harper's Weekly*, March 12, 1887, p. 73; Courtesy Mr. and Mrs. Ivar Axelson, pp. 84, 108, 109, 132–133; Courtesy A. L. Darwin, p. 95; Courtesy Mrs. William J. Krome, p. 98; Thomas Annadown, p. 118; Courtesy Mrs. Frank Brayman, p. 119; Courtesy Glen Simmons, p. 142; Matlack Collection, Historical Association of Southern Florida, p. 146; Courtesy Mrs. Loren Roberts, p. 148; Romer Historic Files, p. 173; Courtesy Miss Thelma Smallwood, p. 176; William M. Stephens, p. 181.

PREFACE

THE DEDICATION of Everglades National Park in 1947 and the determination of its boundaries a decade later fix for the foreseeable future the uses to which this area and its natural resources will be put. The Park is to be preserved in its natural state for the enjoyment and education of all. But as time passes and nature reasserts control of this unique land it will be easy to forget that it was the scene of constantly changing human activities and interests for at least two thousand years.

History is stacked in favor of those who leave records, and few of those who live on isolated frontiers either produce or preserve historical documents of any sort. Fortunately, the physical remains of the aboriginal Indians who lived in the Park are relatively undisturbed and make possible the reconstruction of some of their life histories. Many of the white settlers came out of comparative obscurity, stayed for brief times, and vanished into oblivion, leaving no records whatsoever. A few representative stories of those people who made lasting impressions upon visitors and of others who by chance or design left some records of their lives are included here. Others appear because a few first and second generation permanent residents of the region are still living and it is their accounts of the past that give added authenticity to this narrative.

Over the past fifteen years I have visited these people, shared at least vicariously many of their experiences, and learned to understand their appreciation of what their sometimes precarious lives meant to them. That I share with them some degree of sentimentality and nostalgia is freely conceded.

CHARLTON W. TEBEAU

Coral Gables, Florida
December, 1967

ACKNOWLEDGMENTS

MANY PERSONS have had a part in this effort to present the story of man in the Everglades National Park area. Special thanks are due to the staff of Everglades National Park for their encouragement and assistance; policy makes it impossible to single them out by name. Much of the expense of gathering materials and preparing illustrations was underwritten by a grant to the University of Miami in 1950 by the sons of Barron G. Collier, in honor of David Graham Copeland. This is the third volume in the series entitled "Copeland Studies in Florida History." The illustrations come from numerous sources which are acknowledged on page 9. J. Floyd Monk made a new set of maps for this revised edition.

A number of persons have read parts or all of the manuscript and have added materially to the content as well as saving the author from error. They include Mr. and Mrs. Ivar Axelson, Charles M. Brookfield, Ripley P. Bullen, Frank C. Craighead, John W. Griffin, Mrs. William J. Krome, Miss Deanne Malpass, Albert B. Manly, J. Floyd Monk, Mrs. Julia Morton, Mrs. Loren Roberts, William B. Robertson, Jr., Glen and Maxie Simmons, Charles and Ethel Smith, and Peyton L. Wilson.

Many individuals contributed significant accounts which gave me information and insight into the life of the region. These include Thomas Annadown, Edward Atwell, Mr. and Mrs. Charles T. Boggess, Erben Cook, Arthur Leslie Darwin, Russell G. Frazier, Mr. and Mrs. Leon Hamilton, Eugene Hamilton, Sammy Hamilton, Mrs. Lloyd House, Mrs. Frank Irwin, Mr. and Mrs. Louis Loudon, Mrs. Mary McRae, Ed Moore, Richard Moore, Jack Ozanne, Roy R. Ozmer, Mrs. Laura Conrad Patton, Mrs. Lilly Pent, Joseph Santini, Ted Smallwood, Miss Thelma Smallwood, Hilburn Smith, John Henry Thompson, Mrs. Ed Walker, and Lawrence E. Will. Mr. and Mrs. Ben Archer made available the files of the Homestead *Leader-Enterprise* and its predecessors back to 1912. Mr. G. W. Romer opened his file of the *Illustrated Daily Tab*. The *Collier County News*, the *American Eagle*, the *Miami Metropolis News*, the *Miami Herald*, and *Tropic Magazine* have been sources of useful data.

Finally, my wife, who has gone with me on many field trips and has made many friends among those who lived in the Park, may claim a large share of credit in the writing of this book.

MAN IN THE EVERGLADES

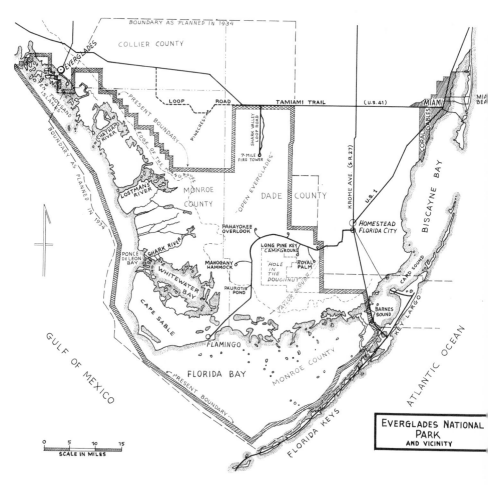

Everglades National Park Boundaries

I   A Subtropical Wilderness

THE UNIQUE NATURAL WEALTH of the lower Florida peninsula has excited the curiosity and imagination and has served the needs of man for at least twenty centuries. Its geographic setting still lures residents and tourists. Yet the Everglades is almost certain to disappoint those who see it for the first time unless they have been prepared for what they may or may not see. As Zane Grey put it in 1924 after extensively examining the area during a fishing trip, "a certain kind of lure began to dawn on me. This was a country that must be understood."

Everglades National Park is at once a limited and a vast sampling of a region full of contrast. It is made up of adjacent, interrelated areas descriptively called the Florida Everglades, the Big Cypress country, the mangrove coast, the Ten Thousand Islands, the Cape, and Florida Bay. The region has nourished—though sometimes harshly—both exotic and familiar flora and fauna. Its people, from the earliest aboriginal Indians to its present day inhabitants, provide clues and records from which the historian can trace the engrossing story of its human history. Such is the aim of this book.

The Park itself consists of over a million acres of land and water, and is our third largest national park. For the purposes of this book the term "Park" will designate only the area within the man-made boundaries, but its story will encompass portions of those areas to the northwest, west, and south that are an essential part of its environmental complex.

It is an area without any single point of powerful impact. Many other national parks that are chiefly of geological interest exhibit great peaks, deep gorges, or spectacular scenes of one kind or another. This Park, which is chiefly of biological interest, requires a different perspective on the part of the visitor.

The geography of Florida, the most southeastern state in the continental United States, is significant. It is bounded by water on three sides—on the east by the Atlantic Ocean, on the south by the Straits of Florida and the Gulf of Mexico, and on the west by the Gulf of Mexico. It has over thirty-five million acres of land and over two million acres of water.

The land here is geologically young, and most of its present topography was created by the actions of interglacial seas surging and receding over the area. The land is also low. Much of the land in the Park is barely above sea level. Fresh water and salt water meet here, mingle, and wash back and forth; in some areas first one and then the other is dominant. This world of half-land, half-water was for centuries so difficult of access that it remained relatively untouched by man. Now its rich wealth of natural resources has proved so attractive that much of it has been exploited almost to the point of depletion.

In its confines the life of the temperate zone meets and mingles with that of the tropics. Strictly speaking the region lies wholly in the temperate zone, but it is so affected by the Gulf Stream, the tropical trade winds, and its latitude that it is termed subtropical. Temperatures range from the torrid highs of the warm wet season from May to November to the occasional ruinous frosts during the cooler dry season. Rainfall may range from thirty to 120 inches yearly. These and other factors make it a region of ecological variety in which change occurs constantly—sometimes subtly, sometimes dramatically—to affect its plant and animal life.

Thus it is now near the northern limit for such animals as the crocodile and the manatee. The crocodile once ranged as far north as Lake Worth and possibly Cape Kennedy. The manatee, or sea cow, is still found occasionally as far north as the mouth of the St. Johns River and very rarely along the coast up to North Carolina. Man's presence in increasing numbers as well as the climate pushed these animals southward.

For the wildcat, gray squirrel, gray fox, black bear, and panther this is near the southern limit of their ranges. They all reach somewhat lower latitudes in Middle America, though there they do not exist so close to sea level as in lower Florida. Similarly, it is the southern limit of such familiar "northern" plants as the hackberry and persimmon, and is the northernmost reach of nearly all of the epiphytic orchids and many ferns which abound in the area.

Differences in the volume of fresh water flowing into the area, fires in seasons of dry weather, and the effects of storms also alter the conditions of life. A difference of a few inches in elevation may change growing conditions so much that a deposit of four or five inches of silt can convert a mangrove area into a buttonwood hammock rising above the surrounding wet lands. Storms may build up or tear down beaches, close inlets, or noticeably alter the coastline. Storms may denude islands of most or all of their plant life and change their animal life entirely. Hurricanes may bring seeds of plants or small animals of Antilles origin to lower Florida.

The Florida Everglades, or "Glades," covering an area of over seven million acres in parts of five Florida counties, is chiefly a great, flat, mostly treeless complex of marshes and wet prairie. This watery land is covered everywhere with its characteristic plant with spiny-edged blades, sawgrass, and is dotted with small tree islands, or bayheads. Hammocks, larger elevated stands of tropical forests, may be found here as well as along the coast and in open pine woods.

Anyone who drives along the Tamiami Trail, U.S. Route 41 just west of Miami, crosses the Everglades. The Park's Seven Mile Tower Road, with access from the Trail, provides an excellent vantage point to view a typical sweep of Everglades terrain. Though it appears to be part of a great level plain nearly thirty miles wide, it is in reality a great drainage basin that has been aptly designated a "River of Grass." The fall in elevation is so slight—from twenty feet at Lake Okeechobee to sea level at its end 150 miles away—that the flow of water is almost imperceptible.

Lake Okeechobee is the largest lake in southern United States. Its seven-hundred square mile area is fed by the waters of the Kissimmee River and other upland streams. Its fresh water once flowed southwestward through the river of grass, or open Glades, to find its way eventually into the Gulf of Mexico. Now the water level of Lake Okeechobee is controlled and its water is stored, used, or diverted by canals and rivers to the Atlantic or Gulf; this and drainage of the upper Everglades has now lowered the water table and greatly reduced the natural flow of water. The Everglades may still be flooded, as such years as 1947 and 1959 showed. However, every gallon of water diverted from the natural flow through the Everglades reduces the water in the Park and alters its natural setting.

On its eastern side the Everglades is separated from the Atlantic Ocean by a coastal ridge. Rivers such as the Miami River at Miami and the New River at Fort Lauderdale cut through this ridge and were part of the natural outflow of Everglades water before the water table in the interior was lowered. Now these rivers are widened and deepened for drainage purposes. The coastal ridge in some measure extends all the way to the end of the Florida peninsula and helps turn most of the Everglades water southwestwardly into the Gulf of Mexico.

A very distinct area with deeper sloughs and ridges stretches along the western side of the Everglades south of the Tamiami Trail and extends to the headwaters of the Shark River. This Tamiami Slough, or Shark River Slough, made it possible to

Seminole in a cypress dugout

travel by canoe or light-draft power boat up the western edge of the Glades to about the Tamiami Trail, and then to Lake Okeechobee or eastwardly to Miami or Fort Lauderdale. On the eastern side the water is more shallow and the outcrop of rock greater, making navigation difficult if not impossible, particularly during dry years.

Equally important in its shorter distance is what is known as Lostman's River Slough, which lies even closer to the western edge of the Everglades. This distinct, shallow basin is clearly observable and runs from about Pinecrest on the Loop, or Chevelier, Road southward to Rock Creek and Lostman's River. Along the way are an unusual number of large hammocks that Indians used frequently as way stations or temporary homesites, the last areas south of the Tamiami Trail to be occupied by Indians. Today Pinecrest, once a settlement large enough to have a school, is a popular place for airboats to be launched and many of the nearby hammock islands are used as overnight or weekend camps for nearby city dwellers.

The open Everglades was a great highway of travel for the aboriginal Indians and their successors in South Florida. Only in driest years, and it should be recognized that there were dry years even before drainage efforts lowered the water table, was travel restricted. White men learned to navigate the river of grass. In the Seminole Wars they used shallow-draft canoes to follow the Indians to their hideouts in the watery region.

More recently white men designed other craft for modern purposes. The glades skiff is a long narrow boat built of boards, somewhat resembling a dugout canoe. The swamp buggy, a sometimes-amphibious craft, is characterized by lightweight, powerful engines, extra low-speed transmissions, and oversized tires. The glades buggy, with caterpillar-type traction, is more commonly used on the eastern side of the Everglades where the larger outcrop of sharp rocks plays havoc with tires or the bottoms of airboats. In the wetter regions of the western Glades the airboat, powered by an airplane propeller, is more common and is equally usable in deeper water where wheeled vehicles cannot operate.

The Tamiami Trail, completed in 1928, bridged the wide river of the Everglades and served further to restrict boat travel

Glades buggy (left), *Swamp buggy* (right)

since it cut directly across many old lines of water traffic. Where the water runs through the restricted areas of the Trail's culverts the flow of water may be quite noticeable; elsewhere it is all but imperceptible. Airboats and swamp buggies are still very much in use in the area but are prohibited in Everglades National Park proper.

The Indian dugout canoe is becoming more and more rare but will probably never be excelled for use under the primitive conditions that prevailed until recently. Its weight, its rounded, narrow shape, and its shallow draft made it possible to paddle and pole through the grassy waters with comparative ease.

On the western side, north and west of the Park boundaries, the Everglades merges into the Big Cypress country, roughly where the Collier–Dade–Monroe county lines intersect near "Forty Mile Bend" on the Tamiami Trail. This area has a slightly higher elevation and its characteristic natural feature is the cypress tree. Today the area rather than the trees is "big." The huge cypress trees that once occupied relatively limited parts of the area in sloughs, swamps, and strands have now largely been removed for lumber. Only the museum stand in Corkscrew Swamp Sanctuary in northern Collier County, administered by the National Audubon Society, remains to show what the virgin cypress forests were once like. The higher cy-

Airboat

press land sharply changes to sawgrass and mangrove along the western and northern Park boundaries.

Mangrove occurs along low-lying tropical seashores throughout the world. The term "mangrove" in a strict ecological sense refers to tropical trees that grow in flooded saline areas. In Florida, mangrove grows on the coast from about St. Augustine southward around the peninsula and up the west coast to about Cedar Key. Florida's southwest coast is peculiarly adapted to mangrove growth, and nowhere in Florida is it so extensive or so well developed as in the Park area. Here on the mangrove

Glades or 'gator skiff

Indian dugout canoe

coast the land merges into the sea and it is difficult to tell if the land is rising out of the water or sinking into it. Mangrove seems to reach its greatest development in areas where its roots are alternately bathed by fresh and salt water, though it is impossible to verify this as an actual cause. The very gradual increase in elevation leaves great areas of the interior affected by the ebb and flow of tides. On the shoreline it appears to stand guard protectively, and in the shallow nearby waters single plants take root to become the nucleus of small islands that may remain independent or later become joined to other islands by expansion and growth.

Three trees in Florida bear the name mangrove—the red, the black, and the white. They belong to three distinct and not very closely allied plant families, and their methods of dealing with the salty environ differ. Physiologists have shown that the red mangrove excludes salt while black and white mangrove excrete it. Red mangrove is clearly recognizable by its extensive prop root system, and the black by the pneumatophores, which resemble asparagus, that its roots send up. The less common white mangrove is not clearly distinguishable but has a characteristical-

Red mangrove

Black mangrove

ly different whitish leaf that is thick and oval-shaped and looks alike on both sides.

These three types of mangrove typically grow in different zones but in the Park they are commonly mixed. The big forest between the coast and the sawgrass country in the Park is roughly fifty per cent red, thirty per cent black, and twenty per cent white, and is not zoned. Red mangrove usually makes up the swamp fringes because it has a more efficient floating seedling, but it is found inland as well. Black mangrove when partly decomposed has a punky quality that makes a good mosquito smudge when burned. It is sometimes used as fuel but because of its rank odor it is commonly used only when buttonwood is not available. Buttonwood, also a mangrove, is usually found somewhat inland from the coastal fringe. It is a rough-barked, usually gnarled and twisted tree whose blossoms and fruits resemble clusters of buttons. The wood is presumably hard enough to be used to make buttons but it is better known as a fuel.

Mangrove and buttonwood have long been important sources of tannin and charcoal in the Orient. In Florida, buttonwood was an important source of firewood and charcoal through the first quarter of the twentieth century. The so-called driftwood gathered along more accessible inland areas, prized chiefly for its weird shapes, is usually storm-killed buttonwood found as weathered wood in wooded areas—seldom on beaches. The thick bark of red mangrove has a high tannic acid content but has largely been unused for this product in Florida. An effort early in this century to commercially work the extensive Shark River forest was abandoned.

Florida's most remarkable stand of mangrove stretches from Little Shark River to north of Lostman's River and extends two to six miles inland along the rivers. The trees grow there in peat soil that is ten to fourteen feet deep, and they reach a height from eighty to one hundred feet with straight unlimbed trunks as much as eighteen or even twenty-four inches in diameter. The bark on these trees ranges from .2 to .7 inches in thickness and averages .4 inches. White and black mangrove do not grow so tall but sometimes reach four feet in diameter.

From Lostman's River northward on the Gulf coast the stand of mangrove is more scattered. There are patches of the tall straight trees, but the more characteristic crossed and twisted short ones are more common. The shallower soils and more rapid rise of elevation from the shoreline limit the growth of mangrove here in extent and size.

The mangrove coast offers considerable resistance to the storms and hurricanes that batter the coast from time to time, but occasionally they are peculiarly destructive in their effects on the mangrove forests. The 1935 hurricane killed most of the mature forest along the mainland coast of Florida Bay and Cape Sable. On the islands of Florida Bay all but low shrubs were defoliated and many of the mangrove fringes were torn away. East of Bear Lake in the Park the three types of mangrove and the buttonwood near Flamingo had been so well developed that the name "Black Forest" had been given to the area; twenty-five years after the storm only a few dead trees remained to mark the spot.

In 1960 hurricane damage was even more severe and widespread. Winds of powerful, slow-moving Hurricane Donna blew for nearly thirty-six hours. Wind reached a sustained velocity of 140 miles per hour and 180 in gusts. Storm tides were twelve feet above normal and the drift line of debris on land rose about eight feet above the ground. The hurricane followed the coastline westward to heavily damage the area from Maderia Bay and Flamingo, around Cape Sable, and up the coast towards Chokoloskee and Everglades.

In the Shark River area a large part of the forest which had escaped the 1935 hurricane was killed. Up to Lostman's River from 50 to 75 per cent of the stately old trees, some of them eighty-five feet high and two feet in diameter, died in an erratic meaningless pattern. From Lostman's River north to Everglades damage ranged from 10 to 25 per cent. The Ten Thousand Islands experienced the eye of the storm and suffered most on the exposed Gulf front, which received the brunt of the force of wind and water. On many of the smaller islands the soil and vegetation were partially washed away. Sand and shell were piled up and washed back into the mangrove to a depth of five feet. Pelican Key (formerly called Bird Key) and Duck Rock, both important bird roosts, suffered extensive damage. Sandy Key in Florida Bay was cut in two. In some instances

Abandoned buttonwood heap for charcoal making

Dead mangrove forest, Shark River, 1960

small islands, often little more than clumps of mangrove, disappeared entirely.

At Cape Sable waves running strong and high washed beach sand inland across the beach and covered the low vegetation. Wind and water together swept the dune area clean and piled debris against the hammocks farther inland. Low ridges, storm-built beachfronts of the past, stood out more clearly on the beachfront; some two dozen of these can still be counted. At the Lostman's River mound, site of Indian and white habitation, beach material was deposited to the rear of the mound in a twelve foot drift as much as six feet deep in places. Absence of artifacts in this location suggests that storms as well as Indians had a role in shaping some of the mounds in the Park.

Storms denude some areas of soil and plants but they also deposit as much as five inches of highly nutritive silt in other places. This may alter the plant succession quite radically and may be as important at times as water level, fire, or frost in its effects.

Until 1960 no reliable data on the effects of hurricanes in the Park had ever been collected. Instead there existed a great volume of hearsay, folklore, and theory. Hurricane Donna spurred the National Park Service to make some scientific observations. Vernon C. "Tommy" Gilbert, a Park naturalist, and Dr. Frank C. Craighead, a retiree of the United States Department of Agriculture who has studied the plant life of the Park since 1951, made a survey of the damage and published the results.

Theories as to cause of storm kill are numerous and fascinating but are not conclusive. The most obvious injury results from trees being whipped, bent, twisted, and shattered for hours at a time. But it seems reasonably clear that more than gross physical damage is involved; the kill of standing trees is apparently site-related. Hammock trees broken and denuded by Hurricane Donna survived, as did most of the buttonwood; trees survived in some places and not in others.

One theory is that electric charges between the storm and the ground pass through the trees as conductors, killing them. Defoliation is another explanation offered, but not all trees stripped of their leaves die. In other instances root systems cease to function or are completely destroyed. The presence of some toxic factor, possibly an excess of hydrogen sulphide generated by anaerobic decomposition of the organic material in the soil, may be the cause. Certainly there is often a strong "rotten egg smell" suggesting the presence of hydrogen sulphide after a storm has passed. Lack of oxygen may also be a factor in loss of root function.

Settling of marl—mud-like calcitic deposits—washed up from the shallow bottom of nearby waters and an excess of sodium chloride also contribute to the conditions in which many trees die. In the latter case, the test for usability of soil on the patches of land once farmed in the region was to taste samples for salt, and to wait until rains washed out most of these traces if the salinity at first seemed too excessive.

When the tangle of debris left after storms becomes dry, as it did in the winter of 1961–62, there is great danger of fire. Very severe fires followed the 1935 hurricane. In the Flamingo area fire swept through the extensive hammocks from Crocodile Point to the Flamingo canal and killed nearly all of the living mahogany, much of which had been storm damaged. What the effect of extensive fire protection, if not complete control, will exert on this natural phenomenon remains to be seen.

The Ten Thousand Islands, which lie off the mangrove coast

from Cape Romano to just north of Lostman's River, were caused partly by a drowned coastline. There are evidences of Indian habitation and former shorelines in areas now submerged as much as four feet. The islands are also made up in part by clumps of mangroves that have grown up on oyster bars in the shallow water, possibly assisted in some instances by storm action.

There are a number of deep, natural channels or passes through the Ten Thousand Islands, including West, Indian Key, Sandfly, Chokoloskee, Rabbit Key, and Fakahatchee. There are also rivers or streams deeper than one would expect. These usually have at their entrances obstructions of sand, mud, or, more likely, oyster bars that may make the entrance of boats difficult. But once inside the rivers or streams these waterways are wide and deep. Their sources are in the fresh water of the Everglades that they drain. In wet weather they carry large volumes of fresh water but in very dry seasons they may be little more than tidal inlets. Though longer than the rivers that drain the Big Cypress area up the coast, they are relatively short since they originate on the edge of the Everglades. Upstream are many intersecting bays that make it possible to move from the headwaters of one to the other. There is no connecting bay between Shark River and Broad River. A channel could be cut to create an inland passage, but many people feel that too much has already been done to change the flow of water—often with unfortunate consequences.

The lower Everglades, a complex of fresh-salt water, mangrove coast, and shallow sea with myriad half-land, half-water islands, forms the vital zone that maintains the vast numbers of birds that inhabit and seasonally visit the region. It supplies food for the bird rookeries of most of the Park, and is the ready source of food for the East River, Cuthbert Lake, and Shark River rookeries.

Duck Rock is a spectacular instance of an offshore island rookery that depended on this zone for food. Prior to Hurricane Donna, which destroyed much of the vegetation on the key, as many as one hundred thousand white ibis came there to roost. American egrets, snowy egrets, several kinds of herons, man-o-war birds, brown pelicans, cormorants, and often as many as three hundred roseate spoonbills once regularly roosted on Duck Rock. Of these only the man-o-war birds do not feed in the Everglades.

After Hurricane Donna about half as many white ibis were counted, indicating that the storm had destroyed great numbers of this outstanding bird population. The bird colonies returned to roost on the broken trees at Duck Rock for two summers after the storm, and then abandoned it, moving to Buzzard Key six miles to the southeast. After one year they moved to the mouth of Chatham River, where they stayed for one season, and then moved inland toward Gopher Key. Duck Rock is now almost without vegetation, a return to its former state when, old timers recall, it was nothing but a bare rock with a lake in the center. Here ducks were shot and from this the key was named. Boat tours from Everglades National Park used to make regular trips to the spectacular bird display at Duck Rock; these tours have now been diverted to view roosts in Chokoloskee Bay.

Cape Sable is composed of three points of land—East Cape, Middle Cape, and Northwest Cape—collectively called "the Cape." The sand beach, which extends along the shore for the greater part of its entire distance, is in reality a series of sand and shell dunes built up by tidal currents and hurricanes. The sand separates the Gulf waters from the characteristic marl prairie, grassy but treeless, which lies behind it. In the Flamingo region the marl prairie reaches out into Florida Bay in the form of mud flats without any sand fringe.

The Cape and the prairie behind it are part of a distinct natural area isolated from the rest of the peninsula by marshes, swamps, and Whitewater Bay. The narrow marl prairie commences at its eastern end near Flamingo and broadens out to cover a wide area westward across the tip of Florida. It is a distinct ecological unit as well as being the lower end of the coastal ridge that turns the waters of the Everglades toward the Gulf of Mexico. It should not be confused with the sawgrass prairie of the Everglades. The marl prairie was originally so high in elevation that only its inner edge was ever flooded by water coming down through the Glades. Drainage canals have now been cut through it. An old road once crossed the prairie from Flamingo, touching the coast near Big Sable Creek.

A somewhat different area stretches from Flamingo east to U.S. Highway 1. Its drainage is away from the coastal ridge to the east. There is the usual fringe of mangrove on the shore, beyond which there is a low coastal ridge with buttonwood hammocks and an occasional patch of higher, dry prairie. As one moves inland there is a string of mangrove-enclosed lakes, of which Cuthbert Lake and West Lake are best known. Finally, when approaching the true coastal ridge, there is sawgrass prairie dotted with tree islands, botanically quite similar to the edges of the Everglades on the north side of the same rock ridge. This area can be seen south of Florida City on the road to the Park entrance or on the highway to the Florida Keys.

The famed Florida mahogany, sometimes called madeira, grew principally in hammocks between Flamingo and Madeira Bay. This tree has a long trunk with straight grain, and may grow to four feet in diameter and stretch forty feet to the first limb. Mahoganies are not fire resistant, and the 1935 hurricane and the fires that followed left so few of them that they no longer reseed naturally. Since National Park Service policy views this as a natural condition no effort is being made to restore them. Foresters now gather the seed of the few remaining stands at some distance in the interior at Mahogany Hammock, and on northern Key Largo, for experimental plantings in the West Indies and as far south as Puerto Rico. The mahogany's high-quality wood was used for fine lumber in the Spanish and British periods of Florida history. An excellent remnant of the great hardwood forest spared by storm, fire, and timber cutters may be seen just west of the road to Flamingo on the Mahogany Hammock Trail in Everglades National Park.

The whole area from Flamingo to Shark River was referred to by early Floridians as "down at the Cape." How the name Cape Sable originated is something of a mystery, although it may be translated from the French as "sandy cape." It may have been named for the sabal palms that once grew there. Until late in the nineteenth century, Middle Cape was called Palm Point after a stand of coconut trees growing there. There are repeated but unconfirmed reports of two very tall royal palms that grew there and served as landmarks of such importance to sailors that they were reportedly protected by law. References

by sailors to Cape Sable undoubtedly referred to Middle Cape.
Later in the 1880's a large commercial coconut palm grove was
planted on Middle Cape.

The Florida Bay area of the Gulf of Mexico between the
Florida Keys and the southwest coast of the mainland is a region
of shallow bays and sounds dotted with mangrove islands or
keys, which range in size from mere clumps of mangrove bushes
to nearly one hundred acres. During low tide much of the sea
floor is exposed as miles of "banks" or "mud flats" that provide feeding grounds for thousands of birds. Many channels and
passes lead maze-like through the shallow sea area, forming
challenging but reliable water routes for small boats engaged in
fishing or birdwatching—for which the area is justly famed. An
area of 370,000 acres of Florida Bay is included within the
Park boundaries largely to protect birds and their feeding
grounds.

The eleven islands that comprise the Dry Tortugas, located
about seventy miles west of Key West at the westernmost end of
the Florida Keys, although geographically separated from the
Park are properly a part of this story. Fort Jefferson National
Monument on Garden Key is administered by the superintendent of Everglades National Park. The Tortugas are the best
known nesting place of sooty and, to a lesser degree, other terns
in the United States, and the islands have been under federal
protection since early in this century.

The low-lying Tortugas islands, except for Garden and Loggerhead keys, are subject to flooding by storm tides. Early
mariners frequently visited these keys to collect sea birds, turtles,
and the now extinct, or nearly so, West Indian seals for ships'
food supplies. Others came from as far away as Havana to
gather eggs at nesting time. John James Audubon in 1832 reported sooty terns in great numbers on Bird Key and noddy
terns on Bush Key. Eggers from Havana collected a cargo of
what they said was eight tons of eggs that would be sold at
home for seventy-five cents a gallon. Eggers are assumed to have
driven sooty and brown noddy terns from East Key where they
nested until late in the nineteenth century.

Much of the history of the Tortugas is associated with military occupation. Garden Key, with its adjacent protected an-

chorage, had a lighthouse by 1825 and the construction there of
Fort Jefferson began in 1846. Hospital Key (formerly Sand
Key), a small, shifting sandbar with little vegetation, was utilized
for isolation of yellow fever patients in the 1860's. Bush Key,
where most of the sooties and noddies have nested in recent
years, was the pasture and slaughter ground for cattle and hogs
brought in for the garrison. This once well-vegetated key disappeared in an 1870 hurricane but gradually reappeared and is now
second largest of the islands. Bird Key, the principal nesting
ground for sooty terns and brown noddies until it washed away
in the 1930's after much gradual erosion, was a hospital site, a
quarantine station, and a cemetery. Loggerhead Key, largest,
highest, most vegetated, and perhaps best known as the site of
Loggerhead Light, built in 1856–60, is not important as a nesting site.

The crowded and noisy breeding colonies of sooty terns far
outnumber others and attract most attention. They have fluctu-
ated from a low of about 5,000 adults in 1903 to a peak of
190,000 in 1950, but remained steady at about 100,000 from
1960 to 1964. The brown noddy population dropped from a
high of 35,000 in 1919 to a low of 400 in 1938, and recovered
to about 2,000 in 1964. A small colony of about 150 to 450
roseate terns have also nested there recently. About 500 least
terns nested regularly from 1916 to 1932, dwindled to a few
pairs by 1937, and then disappeared. Royal and sandwich
terns nested abundantly in the mid-nineteenth century but were
apparently extirpated by eggers. No verifiable evidence exists
for the several-times reported nesting of common terns. Black
noddy terns, first reported for the United States in 1960, have
been found there each summer since.

On April 6, 1908 President Theodore Roosevelt established
Tortugas Keys Reservation to protect the birds nesting there.
After that date the Bureau of Biological Survey and the National
Audubon Society began to provide warden protection. The
second President Roosevelt in 1935 declared Fort Jefferson a
national monument and turned it over to the National Park
Service. When Everglades National Park was created in 1947
Fort Jefferson Monument was attached to it for administration.

In the Park itself, the surrounding areas more than the open

Everglades first attracted man to the region. Birds and game fed throughout the Glades, but birds roosted and nested elsewhere and animals found greater security from hunters in hammocks. Hunters often set fire to the hammocks to drive game out into the open Glades. Hammocks also provided some timber, and Seminole Indians cleared fields on the larger, higher ones for limited farming. Paradise Key, or Royal Palm Hammock, is the largest of the Everglades hammocks and is higher and more rocky than most. It was once surrounded by water and thus protected from fire. Only Pine Island, actually an Everglades key, is larger, but it has less the character of a typical Everglades hammock.

Aboriginal Indians were apparently attracted mostly by the great beds of conchs, oysters, and clams in the Ten Thousand Islands area, and made their homes on the islands or on the river banks and hammocks nearby. They also utilized the abundance of fish, wildlife, and plant food available. To the Semi-

Sooty Terns resting on storm drift; Bush Key, Dry Tortugas

noles who came after the early Indians, the region was used primarily as a hunting ground where they shot plume birds in season, killed alligators, crocodiles, and other animals for skins, and hunted deer for hides as well as for food. The white men who followed were primarily hunters and fishermen, but others soon came to cut the cypress and mahogany trees, remove royal palms to beautify nearby urban communities, and farm on the limited land available. Archaeologists and anthropologists also came to seek the remains of early man; naturalists studied the wealth of unique flora and fauna; and collectors of wild orchids, tree snails, and other rare species pushed deeper and deeper into the Park's wilderness.

II Glades Indians—Calusa, Tequesta, and Seminole

FLORIDA'S ABORIGINAL INDIANS included the Apalachee, Timucan, Ais, Jeaga, Tequesta, and Calusa. Of these only the latter two were at home on the lower peninsula. There they developed a way of life considerably different from Indians of North Florida, but anthropologists generally agree that they are of the same origin. Comparative isolation and differences of climate and natural resources are sufficient to explain the distinctive features of the South Florida Indian culture.

It is sometimes mistakenly concluded that these Indians came from the West Indies as did much of the tropical wildlife in the Park. However, it is quite certain that the ancestors of the Park's first human inhabitants began to move from the southeast down into North Florida at least ten, and possibly as much as twenty, thousand years ago, and that by the beginning of the Christian era they had spread slowly down the peninsula to begin an occupation of nearly two thousand years in the Everglades region.

The Everglades separated these early dwellers and continued to act as a natural barrier between the people of the two coasts until early in the twentieth century. On the east coast, with their center at the mouth of the Miami River, were the Tequesta (sometimes Tekesta or Chequesta). At the time of the first Spanish explorations in the early 1500's the province of the Tequesta extended as far north as present day Pompano and down to Cape Sable and the Florida Keys.

Don Andreas Gonzales Barcia's invaluable collection of Florida records covering the period of 1515 to 1722 reveals that there was a Tequesta village at what seems likely to have been Cape Sable. Other writers have suggested that the Tequesta dominion extended up the west coast as far as Lostman's River.

It is quite possible that the Tequesta met the west coast Calusa at the lower end of the Everglades, first one and then the other dominant. Archaeological evidence shows more Calusa than Tequesta at the Cape.

The relative importance of the two tribes may be assumed by the numbers estimated to belong to each. The common population figure for the sixteenth century is eight hundred Tequesta and two thousand Calusa, the latter living in some thirty villages.

When the Spaniards arrived the Calusa were certainly in the ascendant. Their principal settlement was somewhere near the mouth of the Caloosahatchee River, and the greater part of the members of both tribes probably lived outside of present Park boundaries. The Calusa appear to have exercised some degree of cultural if not political leadership over most of the Indians south of Lake Okeechobee. In fact, the Tequesta are sometimes misidentified as Calusa in literature.

Both groups relied upon the natural food resources of the area, primarily shellfish and fish supplemented with game and wild plants. In few other areas could people live the year around by fishing, hunting, and gathering wild plants without migrating from place to place. Only on the north Pacific coast is there a comparable non-agricultural food supply. In Florida the greatest concentration of this food supply was on the west coast, and there the Indian culture reached its greatest richness and diversity.

Archaeologists for their purposes designate the region of subtropical Florida the Glades Area, and the Indians whose culture reflects this environmental influence as Glades Indians. Anthropologists describe the pottery that these Indians made and used as gritty and hard, and of good quality for its utilitarian purposes. Decoration was often lacking, and when present was never elaborate. For the Glades Indians a few lines of incising near the vessel rim or some punctations served to decorate the cooking pots. The Indians were consistent enough in the use of certain designs at different times for anthropologists to classify the designs by time periods.

Lacking flint or any other hard stone, or any metal with which to make tools or weapons, the materials at hand—chiefly

Pottery of the Glades Area: a, b, *Glades Tooled;* c, *St. Johns Check Stamped;* d, *Surfside Incised;* e, f, *Key Largo Incised;* g, *Opa Locka Incised;* h, *unclassified incised;* i, *Fort Drum Punctated;* j, *Gordon's Pass Incised;* k, *Miami Incised;* a-c, *Glades III Period (A.D. 1000– 1500);* d, *very late Glades II (ca. A.D. 1000);* e.k., *Glades II Period (A.D. 200–1000);* c, *imported from northeast Florida;* i-j, *more prevalent towards the west*

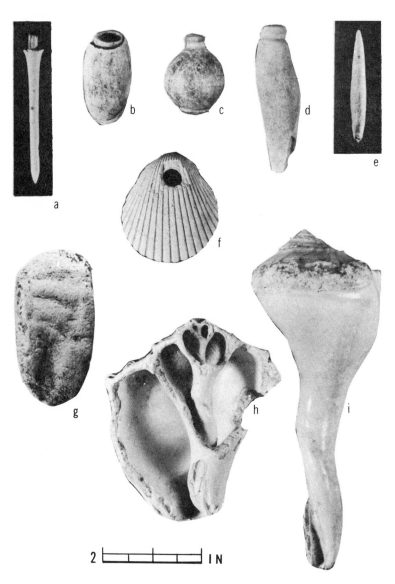

Ornaments and Tools of the Glades Area: a, bone hairpin; b, shell bead; c, d, stone and shell pendants; e, simple bone point; f, shell bead or pendant; g, shell ax; h, shell hammer arranged for hafting; i, shell pounder

shells, bones, wood, and other vegetable fibers—were used. Large conch shells fitted with wooden handles served as cutting, digging, and pounding tools. The Indians made effective knives of sharks' teeth set in wooden handles. Shell and bone ornaments have been collected in considerable numbers, indicating that decorative artifacts were also commonly used.

Villages were usually located at the mouths of rivers or inlets and on offshore islands. Indians traveled freely in the Everglades but rarely lived for any length of time in the open Everglades. They traveled mostly by canoe and though no remains or descriptions exist to guide us, we may reasonably assume that dugout canoes not unlike those used by other southeastern Indians were used in the Glades. There is little evidence of overland travel but signs of canoe trails through the watery region can be traced by middens—refuse heaps marking human habitation—that mark Indian stopping places on the banks of streams and island way stations.

Rookery Mound, a low black dirt midden located on Rookery Branch, a headwater stream of the Shark River, is a good example of a Calusa temporary habitation. John M. Goggin, noted Florida archaeologist and anthropologist, visited this mound in 1950. At that time he described Rookery Branch as "a long mangrove-bordered finger stretching out into the Everglades" that had long been an important waterway from the Glades to the west coast. Rookery Mound is about eighty feet long, thirty to forty feet wide, and only a little more than two feet deep. At the time of Dr. Goggin's visit he found that Seminoles had used the mound recently enough to have left a growth of sugar cane and a few citrus trees. Animal bones unearthed indicated that the Calusa's local food supply included turtles, which evidently were abundant, deer, small mammals, and possibly manatees, as well as fish, alligators, birds, and crabs.

Rookery Branch and Rookery Mound were named for a large bird nesting site on the upper reaches of the stream. Charles M. Brookfield of the Tropical Audubon Society, while guarding the rookery for two months in 1946, discovered the mound. He camped at Little Banana Patch, identified by a clump of banana plants, a place so marshy that it was necessary to lay a floor of boards to support his tent and table. Farther downstream is a larger mound on Avocado Creek, which was named for the mound's evidences of Seminole cultivation including still-growing avocado trees. A pitcher pump there gives evidence of an effort to get fresh water, but none was available in the dry spring of Brookfield's stay.

The Calusa developed a relatively complex social organization. Some lived in villages of two hundred or more. They engaged in such cooperative enterprises as the construction of canals, shellworks, and earthworks, some of the best known examples of which are in or near the Park. These works must have required millions of man hours of labor, time for which was available because of the comparative ease of providing food, clothing, and shelter.

Hernando d'Escalante Fontaneda, a youth of 13 en route from Colombia to Spain to be educated, was shipwrecked on the Florida Reef and lived seventeen years, probably from 1545 to 1562, among the Glades Indians. In his remarkable memoirs written in Spain in 1575 he noted, "These Indians have no gold, less silver and less clothing. They go naked, except only some breech cloths woven of palms, with which the men cover themselves; the women do the like with certain grass that grows on trees. This grass looks like wool, although it is different from it."

From the scanty records and remains of the Calusa we know that their culture included religious festivals and special shamans. The chief, combining certain priestly prerogatives with those of his office, had near absolute power. Spanish priests left descriptions of the ceremonial masks worn by their Calusa counterparts, usually pronouncing them horrible to behold.

The Calusa were so effectively organized for defense that the Spaniards gave up their first efforts to subdue and convert them and transplanted the missions and settlements farther north where the Indians were more docile and tractable. The principal Calusa weapon was the bow and arrow, but they also used clubs and spears, with which they used atlatls, or spear-throwers.

The largest collection of Calusa artifacts was extracted from peat and mud on the mangrove coast of Marco Island in 1896 by the Pepper-Hurst Archaeological Expedition led by Frank

Hamilton Cushing. The site was discovered by an early Marco pioneer, Captain W. D. Collier, in 1895. This find was rare in that wooden objects, some with paint remaining, were found. These included ceremonial masks, a carved deer head, bowls, and boats, as well as tools, utensils, and weapons of other natural materials. The artifacts were preserved in the muck at the Marco site. Persistent search has failed to reveal other such remains in the Ten Thousand Islands region, but it is unlikely that these articles of common use were in any way unique. In 1967 a six-man team headed by L. Ross Morrell, state archaeologist, began a systematic sampling of all remaining mounds at Caxambas on Marco Island, aided by the Collier County Historical Society and the land developers who will shortly erase all evidences of the former Indian culture in the area.

No description of Tequesta houses is available except those on Matecumbe Key described by Bernard Romans, a surveyor for the British government, who wrote ". . . we see the remains of some savage habitations, built, or rather piled up of stones; these were the last refuges of the Caloosa [Tequesta] nation; . . ." This may actually have been a unique instance of the use of stone. The Tequesta probably built some kind of wooden shelters similar to those of the Calusa. Wood and other vegetable fibers and occasionally skins of animals usually were used for building purposes.

Juan Ponce de Leon stopped at a bay he called Chequescha, apparently present day Biscayne Bay, in his voyage of discovery in 1513. Half a century later one of the ships in the fleet of Pedro Menéndez de Avilés, one of Spain's ablest explorers, was caught in a storm and took refuge in Biscayne Bay. The main Tequesta village was located there in 1565, and Menéndez was treated well by the Indians. The Jesuit missionaries with him took the nephew of the Tequesta chief to Havana to be educated. The chief's brother accompanied Menéndez to Spain, where he became a Christian. In 1567 Menéndez again visited the Tequesta and established a mission there protected by a garrison of thirty soldiers. Brother Francisco Villareal, who had learned something of the Tequesta language from the nephew of the chief in Havana, remained to convert the Indians. He felt he was successfully winning over the children and some of the elders until the soldiers, who occasionally provoked acts of hostility, executed an uncle of the chief. The enraged Indians tore down the cross and attacked the garrison, forcing Brother Francisco to abandon the mission for a time. When the chief's brother returned from Spain, friendship was re-established. The Indians replaced the cross and Brother Francisco returned, but in 1570 the mission was abandoned for work in more fruitful fields elsewhere.

A letter written by Brother Francisco in January of 1568 described a plague of mosquitoes of three months duration, during which the only relief was to remain close to the fire smothered in smoke. A majority of the Indians, he reported, had gone to an island a league away to eat coconuts and palm grapes (and perhaps to escape the mosquitoes), leaving not more than thirty of their number at the base. At the time of the missionary's letter Indians from many villages had gathered at a site near present day Miami to build a house for their chief. Brother Francisco reported that their food also included whales and fish.

In his memoirs Fontaneda recalled, "Their common food is fish, turtle and snails, and tunny and whale; . . . Some eat sea-wolves [West Indian seals known to be there in great numbers at the time]; not all of them, for there is a distinction between the higher and lower classes, but the principal persons eat them. There is another fish which we call here *langosta* [lobster], and one like unto a *chapin* [trunkfish], of which they consume not less than of the former."

The Tequesta were skilled and daring fishermen. They chased large fish in their canoes and especially sought the sea cows (manatees), to which delicacy modern white man gave the name "pork of the sea." They used ropes and stakes harpoon-fashion to catch manatees, sharks, sailfish, porpoises, stingrays, and small fish. Also found in the middens of Indians living back from the coast are bones of deer and fresh water turtles. Coastal Indians, like their successors, caught ocean turtles when they came to lay eggs on the beaches. Dan D. Laxson of Hialeah, a local archaeologist who has examined many of the Tequesta middens on the edge of the Everglades, remarked somewhat facetiously that they must have lived principally on turtles if one is to judge by the bones that remain.

Other foods available to the Tequesta were coontie roots, which their Seminole successors and the early white settlers also used extensively, and palmetto berries, fresh and dried. The latter were carried on the trail for food, though the average European preferred near starvation to that Indian delicacy. Cocoplums, sea grapes, prickly pears, and wild figs were also available in season, though some students of the subject doubt that figs were eaten.

In 1743 Fathers Monaco and Alaña, Jesuits from Havana, established a chapel and a fort at the mouth of Rio Ratones, or Little River at present day Fort Lauderdale. By this time the fortunes of the Tequesta were dwindling. Father Monaco reported attacks by raiding bands of the Creeks who later became known as Seminoles. In 1763 when the Spaniards surrendered Florida to the British the missionaries and soldiers departed, never to return, leaving the field to the incoming Seminoles. In the British period which followed, Bernard Romans noted several deserted Tequesta villages, and somewhere picked up the information that eighty families had left with the Spaniards. He, incidentally, referred to all the Indians of the area as Calusa, while in reality these were undoubtedly Tequesta.

The Calusa and all other aboriginal Indians like the Tequesta—except possibly the "Spanish Indians"—were gone from Florida by 1800. White settlers who were on Biscayne Bay by 1820 referred only to Seminoles. The early Indians died primarily of diseases introduced by white men and in the Indian wars; others were carried off into slavery by raiding Creeks and whites. Though the aboriginal Indians had lived in Florida for two thousand years, they left scarcely a place name south of Caloosahatchee—and even in that case the "hatchee" is Muskogean for "river." The whites probably had so little contact with Indians that no names were taken over from them. Spaniards gave names to key coastal areas but few of these were of Indian origin.

The Calusa left an enormously impressive series of monuments to remind us of their long occupation. The huge shell mounds on Florida's west coast and nearby islands mark sites where they lived. In the Park many of these mounds are intact. They are of several types—burial or ceremonial mounds, habitation sites, and simple shell heaps. Farther north some of the mounds have been leveled for building sites or hauled away for street and road building. Visitors can most easily see remnants of these mounds at Marco and Chokoloskee. At two of the three sites on Marco Island—Marco townsite and Caxambas—the original shell mounds have been augmented by a great many clam shells deposited by canneries in this century. At the third site at Goodland on the east point of Marco Island an estimated 150,000 cubic yards of shell have been removed from the mound.

Impressive remains of shell mounds abound on Chokoloskee Island, the southernmost point of Florida's west coast to be reached by highway and surrounded by Park boundaries on three sides. Dredging and leveling operations have revealed the nature and extent of the shell mound, a 135-acre area which rose in some places as much as twenty feet.

An equally impressive and completely intact group of mounds lies on the east bank of the Turner River near its mouth opposite Chokoloskee Island. These thirty or so mounds have excited interest since the beginning of the century when scientists first visited there, and it is hoped that someday these mounds may become part of Everglades National Park.

After the 1896 expedition previously mentioned, Dr. Cushing advanced the theory that mounds were placed on carefully chosen sites to create refuges from high water. William H. Sears, at the time an archaeologist and anthropologist for the Florida State Museum, examined the Turner River mounds in 1955 and concluded that the dry areas were not deliberately created.

He concluded that the shells must have been deposited on submerged and still-growing mud flats under normal high tide level, and that the black middens containing cultural debris were built up at a later date. The midden areas were confined to low spots between mounds and to basal portions of the mounds, with sherds and shell tools found only on the lower slopes. These extended upward four or five feet, above which shell only was found in test pits.

Dr. Goggin reached the same conclusion as Dr. Sears at Goodland, where the middens are confined to low spots between and around the mounds. This conclusion does not, of course, preclude the use of mounds as places of refuge for the original builders, if only temporarily, and it is certain that they were used as such by modern dwellers. Charles G. McKinney of Chokoloskee Island commented after the unusually high water of the 1910 hurricane that he could easily understand why the Indians built up the high mounds.

However, it may be an error to assume that dry land was important to Indians of this region. Dr. Sears concluded that it was certainly not important culturally, for the population with its dwellings appears to have moved seaward away from the growing elevated areas toward the water which supplied food. The Indians formed new dry areas as they moved. The advantage of nearby sources of food may have outweighed the annoyance of insects, the plague of all white settlers. To have lived far enough away to escape the insects might have placed the Indians beyond the easy reach of the shellfish beds. It is also possible that with a generally higher water table there were fewer mosquitoes in some localities.

Whether by accident or by design, the Calusa were great builders of dry land. Mounds are found all along the western border of the Park as far south as Shark River. One on Chatham River is forty acres in extent, and there are sixty acres of ridges and mounds on Dismal Key. Other large mounds are at Russell Key, Sandfly Island, and Gopher Key; the latter is notable as an extremely large mound and probably the least disturbed of all the shell mounds in the Park.

Many other mounds are quite limited in extent, probably indicating temporary occupation. Nearly all mounds constituting an acre or more have at one time or another been cultivated if not inhabited by white men. Dr. Craighead, who has visited most of the mounds, says he has never found one without some signs of cultivation.

The number, extensive area, and depth of the shell in the

mounds pose many questions. One wonders if the number of Indians was not larger than is commonly supposed; whether the middens were merely refuse heaps, as most anthropologists believe, or were designed to raise some areas above the reach of storms; or whether the mounds originated as refuse heaps and later evolved into carefully executed structures when their usefulness was realized. On the western side of the Park the existing mounds constitute almost the only high land. The Lostman's River ranger station of the National Park Service stands on a shell mound occupied for half a century by white men before it became part of Park property.

Shells for the mounds were plentiful, for the shallow waters of the Ten Thousand Islands teem with shellfish. Oysters abound in the brackish waters of the bays where fresh water from the Everglades enters, but oysters never had commercial importance in Florida. Farther out among the islands and in the shallow sea, particularly from Rabbit Key southward, clams were once found in great numbers and were the source of supply for two canneries on Marco Island in the first half of this century. Today, after being depleted, clams are hopefully but mistakenly reported to be "coming back" in commercial quantities.

In the interior, away from the coastal shell mounds and usually in association with a nearby watercourse, other mounds mark overnight Indian stands and temporary occupation. Many of these are mere refuse heaps, or middens. Others are earth mounds, there being no nearby deposits of shell. If shell mounds are only refuse heaps, as is commonly maintained, how shall we account for such earth mounds?

One earth mound of extraordinary proportions—and fortunately of easy access—is Bear Lake Mound, which lies just east of Bear Lake within a few miles of Flamingo. It is some four hundred feet long and thirty feet wide, and standing on its ridge one can see out atop the surrounding mangroves. Some two dozen majestic royal palms grew there amid the thick tropical hammock until destroyed by a hurricane. Preliminary investigations reveal that this mound was once on the shore, and an overlay of charcoal over the foundation shell shows that it was also at one time a living site.

Associated with this mound is Bear Lake Indian Canal, near

the modern day Homestead Canal dredged directly eastward. The old canal's course is discernible, running southeastwardly toward Florida Bay. It apparently once provided access to Bear Lake. It was twenty to thirty feet wide and one to two feet deep—enough to accommodate Indian canoes. Archaeologist Clarence B. Moore noted small middens along its banks in about 1900. It is now completely overgrown with mangroves and other plants, but its course out to Florida Bay can be followed on an aerial survey map. It is not unlike the course of a mangrove creek except that it was remarkably straight, and it may well have followed the course of such a stream. Skeptics maintain that it may have been merely a mangrove creek.

Bear Lake Indian Canal would have required deepening for use only in dry times when the level of Everglades water that fed it fell below the natural level of the Creek. It may have been tidal to some extent. It would have provided canoe travelers from the Ten Thousand Islands or the western Everglades a shorter and protected way through Coot Bay to Mud Lake, and thence to Bear Lake and out to Florida Bay. Otherwise one had to go all the way around the exposed Cape Sable route.

The last of the mound-building, if not mound-dwelling, Indians departed with the Spaniards when Florida was surrendered to the British in 1763. None returned when Spain again took temporary possession of Florida from 1784 to 1821.

Seminole Indians moved into Florida to occupy the area being vacated by its earlier inhabitants. They arrived in increasing numbers after 1700, partly in response to the natural attractions of the unoccupied North Florida region and partly as a result of the pressure of English settlements in Carolina and Georgia. These Indians were mostly settlers from the Creek Confederacy, a large, loosely organized group that included some Creeks and several other linguistic and political groups. Hichiti-speaking Indians such as Oconee and Mikasuki were the major element in the eighteenth century Seminole migration.

There was another extensive migration into Florida at the end of the Creek War of 1812–1814, when the United States government induced the Indians to cede by treaty extensive lands in Alabama and Georgia. After Andrew Jackson defeated the Creeks at Horseshoe Bend in 1814, the defeated Red Stick faction provided enough Muskogee immigrants to Florida for them to outnumber the Hitchiti-speaking bands already there.

In 1821 the treaty ceding Florida to the United States was ratified. By this time some five thousand Seminoles had replaced the twenty-five thousand predecessors who had occupied the state. Generally speaking the Seminoles first settled in North Florida, but there were soon villages as far south as Tampa, and hunters found their way to the extreme southern region. In 1823 at the Moultrie Creek Treaty conference near St. Augustine, the Indians agreed to accept a reservation of five million acres north of Lake Okeechobee but ranged far south of the reservation. In 1830 Congress decreed that all Indians should be removed to lands west of the Mississippi River "far beyond the possibility of any contact with white men." How the Park area was affected by the Wars of Indian Removal is described in the next chapter.

Early writers reported hunting parties on the southwest coast in contact with fishermen from Havana (Bernard Romans, 1775), and trading and hunting expeditions to the seacoast and Keys "quite to the point of Florida" and sometimes to the Bahamas and Cuba (William Bartram, 1791). In 1823 Charles Vignoles counted three hundred Seminoles in the Cape Florida area, some of them brought from Cape Sable by Bahama wreckers. They traveled around the coast from Cape Florida to Charlotte Harbor, which might suggest that they knew little about the interior of the peninsula. This seems unlikely, however, since they proved to be so much at home in the southern Everglades area a generation later.

John Lee Williams reported seeing a deserted Seminole village in September, 1832 near Cape Sable. In the same month he met an Indian there on his way to trade at Indian Key on the lower east coast.

Seminoles, unlike the Tequesta and Calusa, were not generally a coastal-dwelling people. They were primarily agriculturists, supplementing gardening with hunting as did other Indian groups in southeastern United States. They had begun to raise cattle and otherwise to borrow white man's ways. The Seminoles had lived in larger settled villages until they retreated southward; there the social organization broke into smaller

Seminole chickee, about 1920

bands. They continued to plant gardens, keep a few hogs, and sometimes a few head of cattle even though land suitable for agriculture became scarcer and their livestock less safe on the open range.

Perhaps the principal change made by the Seminoles as they moved southward was more reliance upon hunting for food and money. There was a ready market for hides, furs, and feathers, and Seminoles ranged far afield in search of game, also using the meat for food. They also adopted the open-sided platform house with palm-thatched roof, possibly copied from those of the Calusa. These were almost certainly some sort of adaptation rather than an invention, and were much better suited to the climate than the more substantial houses they had lived in before migrating to Florida.

The Seminoles did not make permanent homes in South Florida until driven to do so in the Seminole Wars. Their last stand was largely in the Big Cypress country in present day Collier, Hendry, and Lee counties northwest of the Park. United States armed forces seeking Indian hiding places during the wars visited and searched most of the area south of the present-day Tamiami Trail. They found few if any permanent camps or cultivated fields but many evidences of hunting and overnight campsites on nearly every hammock or river bank that provided a bit of dry land. The soldiers were well aware that the Seminoles moved about the area in their canoes.

White men began to visit the area in greater numbers in the last quarter of the nineteenth century. They reported many Indians hunting in the Shark River—Whitewater Bay area, particularly in the season for taking plume birds for their feathers. The remaining Indians continued to live in almost undisturbed isolation until about 1930. They continued to get most of their income from the sale of hides and furs after the sale of plumes became illegal. They came out occasionally to trade in small parties at Miami and Fort Lauderdale on the east coast and at Chokoloskee, Everglades, Marco, and Fort Myers on the Gulf coast. A map prepared in 1930 by Roy Nash for the Commissioner of Indian Affairs showed nearly a score of Indian camps in Collier County in the Big Cypress area near the Everglades. There was one camp each at Immokalee, Everglades, and the head of Turner River, three camps in Monroe County, and two in Dade County.

A. W. and Julian A. Dimock, who explored, photographed and described lower Florida early in this century, visited some of the above mentioned camps. Their party entered the Everglades by way of Rocky Creek and followed a trail through the grass to Tommy Osceola's camp, only to find it abandoned. They later discovered his new camp, the precise location of which was not disclosed, temporarily abandoned. They described seeing there a sewing machine, a cane mill, and a crude device for distilling, and they visited fields of cane and corn on adjacent keys where every patch of dry land had been cleared and planted. They turned northeast towards Miami and met a Seminole named Miami Jimmy on the trail. They visited his camp and turned back westward after seeing the smoke of civilization from Miami on the coast. They made their way to Tiger Tail Hammock, where they found the sign marking the only Indian store ever known to exist in the region—"Mr. Charley Tiger Tail's Store"—and camped two nights there before making their way northward again.

Charley Tiger Tail had moved lumber to build his store from Miami by canoe during high water in 1902 and 1903. He did a considerable business in ordinary trade goods, and also was known as a whiskey peddler. Indians recognized the "flag" flying from a mast on his canoe before they could see him. A photograph published in 1910 of his establishment on Tiger Tail Hammock shows several buildings with a dock extending out into the water. The store was made of boards but the other buildings were typical chickees. The enterprising storekeeper traded at Chokoloskee and Everglades as well as Miami. His post must have been a gathering place for Indians who hunted southward where there was little or no dry land for campsites. Charley had already gone out of business, reportedly a victim of giving too much credit, when a photographer visited the abandoned site in 1908.

Other Seminoles succeeded Tiger Tail; Old Motlo lived there later, as did Charlie Willie, who raised a family on the hammock. Today at the site one may see the remains of buildings and a substantial three-roller cane mill mounted on a platform made of pine logs, except for an accumulation of rust seemingly ready to be used. It is, however, in all probability a later mill than was there in Tiger Tail's day.

It appears that most of Tiger Tail Hammock was at one time cleared. A magnificent specimen of a dugout canoe lay rotting in the grass and water on the east side of the hammock in the 1960's. In 1950 some commercial frog hunters built there a well-equipped shack known as Coconut Camp, which they used irregularly (and asked others to please keep clean) until Hurricane Donna flooded it in 1960. It has not been rebuilt.

Visitors to the region recall that a Seminole medicine man named Doctor Tiger lived on a smaller hammock about two miles south of Pinecrest. These higher islands in Lostman's Slough just north of Park boundaries must have been the homes of the last Indians in the Everglades south of the Tamiami Trail. Erben Cook of Miami, who was surveying land in that area in the 1920's, recalls one Indian family at Tiger Tail Hammock and another between the Loop Road and the present Tamiami Trail.

The opening of the Tamiami Trail in 1928 might be termed

Doctor Tiger with cane mill and cane patch, about 1917

the crucial factor in ending the Indians' old way of life. The growing scarcity of game and the new conservation laws had brought commercial hunting largely to an end. The profitable trade in feathers had ceased a generation before the Park had become the last stand of the plume birds that had once fed and nested over much of southern Florida. The Seminoles lived undisturbed, usually as squatters, on public and private lands. The state of Florida provided them in 1917 with a 99,200 acre reservation near Shark River, a commendable action but taken long after the most desirable state lands had been otherwise allocated. Since scarcely any of the land was habitable this did nothing to deter the Indian way of life.

Camp Lonesome at the head of Rodgers River was a notable exception. The land there is attractive and at least one Seminole Indian claims to have been born on Onion Key in Lostman's River and to have grown up at his family's home at Camp

Lonesome. Charles M. Brookfield visited there in 1947 and saw well built chickees; no Indians were present but tools and utensils about the camp indicated recent occupancy.

While the Seminoles hunted in the Park area, they showed no disposition to claim exclusive use of its land or water. When the Park was created the state reservation land was exchanged, without protest from the Indians, for an equal sized tract of land in Broward County adjacent to the federal reservation in Hendry County.

When the national park was first projected there was immediate concern about its effect upon the Seminoles. Some suggested it would restore the Indians to their birthright, while others were concerned that they would lose their hunting grounds and so part of their livelihood. Ways of compensation were discussed, and some hoped to induce the Indians to remain in the Park to lend authentic color to the scene and to show tourists around somewhat as they had occasionally guided white hunting parties through the region.

All of this concern was too late. The fate of the Seminoles had already been determined by developments antedating the establishment of the Park. Highways had admitted white men to the region to hunt for sport rather than for a source of food or income. It was the white hunters who protested the loss of hunting rights on the Park lands—one of the largest hunting areas still open to them. Though conservation laws had long been relaxed to allow Indians to hunt for food, the Seminoles had turned elsewhere for their livelihoods and had begun to depend on "store bought" groceries and meats. The dugout canoe, the oxcart, and the horse-drawn wagon gave way to the automobile and the airboat, products of the white man's world that were quickly adapted to Indian needs.

The Seminoles moved onto federal reservations, operated souvenir stands, or became wage earners. They found employment on farms and ranches, at sawmills, and in construction work near the area that had once been their hunting ground. Construction superintendents on the Tamiami Trail in the 1920's found Indians to be the most efficient and reliable workers they could employ. Sam Thompson, a construction contractor in Collier County in the same period, hired Indians to clear the site for the town of Everglades and the right of way for the highway north from there, and to set poles and stretch wire for the telephone line to Immokalee. In extensive fire fighting in the spring of 1962 in the Park, rangers found the Seminoles by far the best fire fighters they could recruit—they were at home in the woods, knew their way around, and performed their duties effectively.

Some Indians appeared in amusement parks in cities to wrestle alligators and otherwise act unlike the wilderness Seminoles. Indeed, the Indians may remain most obviously "Indian" only in those areas that they find economically profitable. The souvenir business seems most likely to keep alive certain aspects of Indian culture, to revive some almost forgotten arts, and even to create new ones to satisfy the curiosity of visitors. Two very obvious cultural survivals noticeable in the roadside Indian villages are the open-sided chickees and the colorful dress. At this writing the men have not gone back to wearing the belted shirts of old, nor have they begun the practice of "chiefing" seen in other parks where Indians display themselves and their arts.

The souvenir trade is the basis of a new craftwork industry and is a major source of income for the Tamiami Mikasuki Seminoles. Women do most of the making of souvenir items— skirts (a modification of the Seminole costume), men's shirts, aprons, handbags, grass baskets, dolls of palmetto and coconut fibers dressed Seminole style, pin cushions, and other small articles. Men carve model canoes, wooden spoons, small bows and arrows, wooden tomahawks, miniature totem poles, model birds, tom-toms, and the like; of these only the canoe and the spoons are based on types used by the Seminoles. Seminole artifacts in the museums in the Park and elsewhere are mute evidence of a life that had largely ceased to exist before the Park began.

Present day Seminoles live mainly on three federal reservations some distance from the Park. On the small Dania Reservation twenty miles north of Miami some 150 Indians use or lease 445 acres. On the Brighton Reservation northwest of Lake Okeechobee about the same number manage cattle herds on 36,925 acres of land. The Big Cypress Reservation in Hendry

County south of Lake Okeechobee is located on the edge of the Everglades in Big Cypress country. This 42,663 acre region is the home of about one hundred permanent residents engaged in cattle raising. Here, as on the other reservations, other Indians come and go at will. West of the Big Cypress Reservation and located mostly in the Everglades is a state reservation of 104,800 acres, largely swamp and marsh and not much occupied or used. Much of this area is included in the comprehensive water control plan of the Everglades Drainage District, but this represents no real loss to the Indians, who received the land in compensation for the former state reservation on land now included in the Everglades National Park.

Visitors to the Park are likely to see Seminole Indians at souvenir stands along the Tamiami Trail west of Miami. There is a Mikasuki Restaurant on the Trail near the Seven Mile Tower turnoff to the Park. An educational center maintained by the Indian service is located nearby.

Dr. William C. Sturtevant of the Bureau of American Ethnology at the Smithsonian Institution reminded us in 1958 that language and social organization continued to be strong survivals of the old Seminole culture. The Seminoles were, he wrote, "by far the least acculturated Indians east of the Mississippi and rank among the least acculturated in the United States today." But more recent developments make the rapid breakdown of the last vestiges of Indian culture almost certain. Even those who live on reservations do not escape increasing contact with whites, and in the schools and homes provided for the Seminoles the next generations will lose much of the heritage of their forefathers.

III Exploration and Indian Removal

INDIANS MOVED throughout South Florida for some two thousand years before white men appeared. Spaniards from nearby Cuba and other bases visited the coastal settlements of the Calusa and the Tequesta in the sixteenth century, and there must have been official visits and trading expeditions from Spanish settlements on both coasts. Some Spanish trade goods were probably brought in by the Indians themselves, for they went in their canoes at least as far as Cuba. Seminoles knew their way to the end of the peninsula before the end of the Spanish period of Florida history.

Thanks to archaeologists and anthropologists, we know more about the Indians than we do of the early activities of white men in lower Florida. The coast was mapped after a fashion and reasonably well known on a limited scale by the time Florida became part of the United States, but the information was not widely disseminated. Much of it was in Spanish and buried somewhere in Spain's official archives, where large amounts of it may still remain undisturbed. Thus we have had access only to such fragments as the Fontaneda memoirs, an occasional map, and records of missionaries from the Spanish era in southern Florida.

Spanish Florida included a large portion of the southeastern part of the present United States. After its discovery by Ponce de Leon in 1513, settlements proved most successful in the northern Florida area. St. Augustine was established in 1565, Pensacola in 1698, and a smaller garrison and settlement at St. Marks a few years earlier. The extensive chain of Franciscan missions stretched westward from St. Augustine to about present day Tallahassee and northward from the same base into Georgia until destroyed by raids from Carolina in 1702 and 1704.

In their twenty years of occupation of Florida, from 1763–

1783, the British divided the province into East and West Florida and extended the boundary westward to the Mississippi River. Like the Spaniards before them, the British concentrated their attention in the extreme northeast and northwest portions of the province. Several Britishers explored parts of Florida and published reports, but their references to South Florida were limited or non-existent. Only Bernard Romans, previously cited, made extensive comments on the lower peninsula.

The British retroceded the Floridas to Spain in 1783, but the second Spanish period was only nominally Spanish and the influence and pressure of the United States increased steadily. In 1811 the Americans occupied the region west of the present boundary of Florida as a part of the Louisiana Purchase of 1803. Andrew Jackson occupied Pensacola briefly in 1814 to drive out the British who had moved in during the War of 1812. In 1818 Jackson returned to Florida in a punitive raid, sometimes called the First Seminole War, against Seminoles who menaced white settlers on the international border. In 1819 the United States signed a treaty to acquire Florida from Spain, agreeing to pay five million dollars in claims of American citizens against Spain. The cession took place in 1821 when the treaty was finally signed.

The recently published papers of the territorial period of Florida history show that both Spanish and British fishermen knew the southwest coast if not the interior. In 1824, W. G. D. Worthington, Secretary and Acting Governor of East Florida, reported to the Secretary of State of the United States that eight or nine fishing smacks from thirty-eight to forty tons, believed to be Americans under Spanish license, were fishing off Cape Sable and selling the catch in Havana, and that Englishmen from New Providence were taking quantities of the finest turtle. Worthington thought that American citizens should have a monopoly on the turtling and fishing. Besides that, British fishermen sometimes took part in the marine salvage, or "wrecking," business on the Florida Reef on the Atlantic side of the peninsula, and Spaniards were suspected of maintaining close contact with the Seminole Indians.

Uninformed and naïve public officials quite logically concluded that a road should be constructed along the west coast from

Cape Sable, passing Charlotte Harbor and Tampa Bay to the point where the road (the old Spanish trail) from Pensacola to St. Augustine crossed the Suwannee River. A similar road was projected from Cape Sable northward along the east coast. In February of 1823 Congress authorized the survey. In April of 1824 the Quartermaster General ordered Captain Isaac Clark, assistant quartermaster at Tampa Bay, to survey the route and mark it "by cutting, or as it is called in the Western Country blazing, trees at convenient distances, so that the troops ordered to open the road may trace the route without the aid of a guide."

Such a survey would have provided much useful data, but it was never completed. After progressing as far south as Charlotte Harbor on the west coast, Captain Clark abandoned the survey for want of provisions, and reported that it was impracticable to go any farther even if he had supplies. In August of 1825 Colonel James Gadsen, charged with the survey on the east coast, reported that the population on a road south of New Smyrna would "probably be insufficient to contribute to this

Indian canoe under sail

important object; while the inducements to individuals to keep up the necessary ferries will scarcely ever be adequate." Another person ventured the opinion that only those interested in fishing and wrecking would ever live there.

Wrecking had become a major industry all along the lower coast of Florida, and continued to be so until adequate lighthouses were built to warn ships away from the nearby reef and until military action stopped the pirates of many nations who preyed on the fleets using the shipping lanes just off the coast. Key West, the wrecking center in the early 1820's, evaluated that year's salvage at over two-hundred thousand dollars—and the peak was yet to come.

Dr. Benjamin B. Strobel settled in Key West in 1829 as assistant surgeon to the army post; he later engaged in general medical practice among the townspeople and for a few months edited and published the *Key West Gazette*. One of his first military duties that fall had been to seek out a source of sand suitable for making mortar. He explored most of the Florida Keys north to Biscayne Bay before he found the sand he needed, and while the sand was being loaded he secured a boat and an oarsman from John W. DuBose, keeper of the Key Biscayne lighthouse, and made a trip up the Miami River. He described the Everglades as "an immense tract of country, lying in the middle of the Southern portion of the peninsula. At certain seasons the whole of this region is laid under water, excepting, of course, the higher points of land which then constitute so many islands." He also referred to the region as a lake "for so it might be called under such circumstances." He did not penetrate far enough inland to learn very much, but the captain of a wrecker told him that he had once during high water sailed three days in a northerly direction on a fair wind without discovering any bounds in that direction, and he heard of another person who had sailed in a westerly direction from New River for two days without reaching the western side. Indians, he remarked, traversed the area in all directions.

Strobel left Key West in September of 1832 and went to New York to sell his services to the Florida Peninsular Land Company, which had an option on a tract of land from Cape Sable to Tampa Bay. His petition was successful and he was part of the company's surveying expedition that left Key West in 1833.

Indian Key was an official port of entry and an important trading post between settlements at Key West and Biscayne Bay, and was made the county seat when Dade County was created in 1836. A small naval station was situated nearby at Tea Table Key. Indian Key was the scene of an Indian attack which was the catalyst for one of the most successful invasions of the southern Everglades by United States troops. It was the home of Dr. Henry Perrine, former U.S. consul to Yucatan and noted agriculturalist. Perrine planned to introduce tropical plants into southern Florida and was granted a township of land for that purpose. He may well have visited the Everglades. In the 1830's, after studying temperature records kept for him at Havana, Key West and Indian Key, he developed an organized plan for a settlement at Cape Sable. He notified the General Land Office that he had selected a tract "eastward of Cape Sable . . . and northward of the sandy islands . . ." and requested that it be surveyed under his direction. This was never done. Part of his dream was the construction of a canal from the enormous reservoir of Everglades water in the interior through the relatively high land at the Cape to provide water power for the colony of free white settlers he envisioned in the area. He wanted nothing to do with slavery. Whatever knowledge of the interior he had died with him in the massacre at Indian Key in August of 1840.

The Seminole Wars of 1835-1842 and 1855-1859 brought the southern end of the peninsula sharply to the attention of the United States. The conflict originated in North Florida and the center of activity moved steadily southward throughout the whole episode, the last acts in the drama being played in the Big Cypress country northwest of the Park boundaries.

Before most of the Indians were pushed southward there were some threats to scattered settlements on the lower east coast. Fort Dallas on the Miami River was established in 1837, partly to protect settlers and partly to serve as bases from which to penetrate the interior on Indian hunting expeditions.

Florida's interior was almost completely unknown before this time when thorough exploration, some rather crude maps, and considerable information in official reports and in occasional newspaper and periodical accounts began to appear. Partly because there was so little interest in Florida's past during the half century after the Indian wars these data, mostly unpublished, were largely forgotten.

John Lee Williams, in the Preface of the 1837 edition of his famous *Territory of Florida*, wrote, "The outline south of Tampa Bay and Indian River, I have been unable to fill up. The interior of the territory is wholly unexplored by white men. . . . When I explored the coast my force was not sufficient to ascend the large rivers that enter the Gulf of Mexico, and the great lakes that are believed to supply these rivers are wholly unknown to me." As to Shark River, "which occupies so conspicuous a place in most of our maps, I have omitted because I couldn't find it."

Williams reported several well cultivated plantations in the vicinity of Caxambas Pass, probably at Goodland and at Cape Romano, and a number of boats guided by native pilots going through the pass to avoid the longer and rougher passage around the Cape Romano shoals, which extend southward into the Gulf of Mexico some ten miles.

The notion of a large lake or lakes in the interior that fed the west coast rivers persisted in spite of the information to the contrary available after the Indian wars. In 1857 a Key West contributor speculated in an item in the *National Intelligencer* that a new vent or river had broken out from these interior lakes into the Gulf of Mexico. Basing his assumption on quantities of fresh water in Florida Bay, he calculated that the vent must be somewhere in the neighborhood of Gallivan's Bay.

A Spanish map of the Miami River region dated 1743 supported the idea of a large interior lake dotted with small islands and separated from the Atlantic Ocean by the coastal ridge as we know it today. No rivers were known to flow into this area and a larger number were known to flow out; this logically raised questions about the source of water until the nature of the Everglades drainage basin became known.

Efforts continued to attempt to locate the Indians on the southwest coast who were believed to be purchasing guns and powder from Cuban fishermen. Pursuit of these Indians led to some probing along the unexplored and uncharted waters, with occasional inland journeys on the mainland as far as Cape Sable.

Such an expedition was led by Surgeon General Thomas Lawson, who left Fort Denaud on the Caloosahatchee River in early February of 1838 with 240 officers and men. They made their way by boat out to the mouth of the river and southward to Marco River. Failing to make headway up that stream, they moved to Cape Romano and encamped where there had been a settlement. The next day exploring parties went out in all directions. One party camped on an island, presumably at Goodland, on which there were two or three hundred acres of cleared land. A second day among the islands and passes produced only perplexed Indian guides who, the commanding officer concluded, were deliberately holding back to avoid exposing Indians they knew to be there. Another try on the third day proved even more disappointing. They found a village long since deserted, but the reporting officer was sure it was "the very place at which the Indians would take part were they in that section of the country."

In three days they had found four places that appeared to have been inhabited, but they found not a living soul nor evidence of any having recently been there. Apparently the "Spanish Indians" had abandoned the area. Only one of the places, Cape Romano, had any fresh water.

Lawson reported all the islands except those immediately on the coast "altogether uninhabitable, being covered with a dense growth of mangrove bushes, and they are either under water, or completely flooded, with mangrove roots running horizontally from five to ten inches above the soil, with oysters hanging on them and on the branches of the trees. Judging from what I saw in my several excursions, I am of the opinion that no Indians have occupied this section of the country for eighteen months, and perhaps not since the commencement of the war, and they do not visit it except by appointment with the Spanish fishermen at which time they receive their supplies of ammunition, etc. etc."

The expedition moved by slow degrees southward along the coast, forced twice to take refuge among the islands to avoid disagreeable weather. At the mouth of Chatham River they dropped anchor. The pilot promised positively that they would find twenty families of Indians, and perhaps others from the interior of the country. They did find a townsite, but it appeared to have been abandoned at least twelve months earlier.

After this failure the officer despaired of finding any Indians on the coast, and requested the captain of the steamboat to make for Cape Sable, which they reached on the 18th and from where Lawson wrote:

> . . . where I am now located and about to erect a fort [named Poinsett after the Secretary of War], we are situated on the third and most Southern Point of the Cape; it is accessible at all times, very defensible, and promises to be a healthy position. The first and second, or more northern and western point, I did not like, for the reason that they were not only very bare of timber with which to built a fort, but also destitute of harbour; whereas this one has a safe anchorage and harbor formed by the Keys around, with plenty of fresh water on it, and withal is the favorite haunt of the turtle and other fish. It is perhaps the most beautiful spot on the whole coast, having a high beach in front, an extensive plain immediately behind, with a dry though thick wood a little further removed to the rear. As there is little or no building timber around, and I have as yet neither horses or proper boats to bring it from a distance, I shall attempt to rear a Fort from the beach; that is with the sand thrown out of a ditch, saplings or split logs as a face, and fascines as a body, raise a curtain to a star figured spot which will baffle the skill of the red men to surmount. . . . We have ascertained that there is an inland passage from Carlos Bay to the east side of Cape Romano, and almost to Cape Sable, for vessels drawing five feet water, and that the whole Coast is full of islands, affording good harbors and safe navigation . . . and I have ascertained also, that none other than Spaniards with the Indians are acquainted with the Coast.

One reasonably wonders what had become of the numerous boats that John Lee Williams found operating in those waters and the local pilots ready to take boats through the shorter and safer inland passage; and whether or not they had been Indians trading with Cuban fishermen who had later departed from United States waters.

It seems clear that many people traveled along the coast, that some of them undoubtedly knew the Ten Thousand Islands and rivers, and very likely hunted and fished there if nothing more. What frustrates the historian is the complete lack of any record as to who they were or what they actually were doing.

Official concern and certainty that the Florida Indians were in communication with Cubans somewhere on the southwest coast also accounted at least in part for the establishment of Fort Harrell on a small rocky hammock at the head of New River. It also served as a base from which the remaining Seminoles were hunted down and pushed deeper into the near impenetrable interior. Like many others, Fort Harrell was probably only a stockade used temporarily as an advanced base and then abandoned. Unfortunately, no records exist to give us more information about it.

Fears of the "Spanish Indians" were by no means groundless. These Indians were predominately Seminoles, with perhaps some Calusa remnants who had no contact with English-speaking white men; they spoke Spanish and dealt exclusively with Spanish-speaking fishermen. Their chief, Chekika (sometimes Chakaika), on August 7, 1840 led seventeen canoe loads of Indians in a raid on Indian Key. They came from Chekika's base on the western edge of the Everglades almost directly west of Miami. They killed Dr. Perrine while his family hid in the turtle crawl under the building. They also killed six other people, looted stores, and burned buildings at will. The wily chief then led his men back across Florida Bay to his wilderness hideout, returning, some say, to Marco River or—more probably—by a more southern route such as Chatham River if not across the Glades directly. He undoubtedly did not go around Cape Sable where soldiers stood guard at Fort Poinsett.

Lieutenant Colonel William S. Harney, who had earlier suffered great indignity at the hands of Chekika's group when they made a surprise raid on his small garrison at a post on the Caloosahatchee River, prepared to avenge these attacks. Harney set out from Fort Dallas at the mouth of the Miami River on the evening of December 4, 1840 with ninety men in sixteen canoes. An anonymous member of that expedition sent an account to the *St. Augustine News;* it appeared on January 8, 1841—certainly one of the first, if not the first, accounts ever published of a trip across the southern Everglades.

Harney's party entered the Everglades by way of the south fork of the Miami River. Finding no island to afford them dry land, they spent the night in their open canoes. On the next day the going was difficult because of the sawgrass and the rocky terrain and shallow water, which forced them to wade and pull their boats much of the way. They began to lose confidence in their Indian guide, but when he insisted that he was on course they consented to follow him. He finally led them to a "low tuft of bushes" about half a mile in circumference that seemed as flooded as all the others. However, in the center was a spot of high land about 150 yards around and an abandoned Indian camp. The unknown reporter was fascinated by several strangler figs growing around the trees near the camp.

On the third day "nothing new presented itself to view except one boundless expanse of sawgrass and water, occasionally interspersed with little islands, all of which are overflowed, but the trees are in a green and flourishing state. No country that I have ever heard of bears any resemblance to it; it seems like a vast sea filled with grass and green trees, and expressly intended as a retreat for the rascally Indian, from which the white man would never seek to drive them."

On the fourth day out the men reached the object of their arduous journey, Chekika's island hideaway. They had traversed about forty miles as the crow flies. They completely surprised the Indians and killed Chekika, hanging his body from a tree as a warning to others. Several days were spent in fruitless search for other Indians before Harney prepared to lead his weary men back to Fort Dallas, not by the way they had come but by the easier if much longer route down the western edge of the Everglades to the Shark River and out to the Gulf of Mexico. They missed the Shark, but discovered another route, thereby naming Harney River. The correspondent described the large cypress swamp for many miles along the western edge of the Glades. The party found plenty of water to float their boats and the writer thanked God "we won't have to wade to another island."

Harney showed the way to successfully follow the Indians into their last hiding places—by using canoes and Indian guides.

Other similar expeditions followed. Lieutenant John T. Mc-Laughlin revisited Chekika's island in mid-January of 1841 and left by way of Harney River. In March, Lieutenant St. George Rodgers came in by way of the Harney and left through Marco River. In October, McLaughlin with two hundred men ascended Shark River and entered the Glades, visited intermediate islands, and reached Chekika's island to rendezvous with Captain Burke of the artillery and sixty seven of his men from Fort Dallas. The combined force then proceeded to Prophet's Landing farther up the west coast of the Glades on the edge of the Big Cypress. Sometimes the water proved too low to navigate, as in January, 1842 when an expedition entering by way of the Shark found too little water and returned by way of the Harney.

In March, 1842, Lieutenant J. B. Marchand left Fort Dallas and entered the Glades, following the mainland southward and westward, searching islands for Indians. He found in one small hammock a large quantity of prepared coontie, deer skins, articles of clothing, and cooking utensils carefully preserved in two small structures recently erected. Shoal water stopped southward progress by canoe and scouting parties went out south and west on foot, examining Long Pine and other Everglades keys. They found signs of Indian travel but no settlements. On their return they found some islands north of Long Key that had at one time been cultivated. They then crossed the Everglades to Shark River and returned by a different route. The official report of the trip expressed the opinion that the Indians must be at Cape Sable. The white man was beginning to become as much at home in the Everglades as the Indian.

Hostilities of the Second Seminole War were terminated in 1842 just when the new tactics were proving so effective. But as long as Indians in any numbers remained in the area, Floridians did not abandon efforts to have them removed. In 1855, ten years after Florida was admitted to the Union as a state on March 3, 1845, fighting broke out again in what is generally termed the Third Seminole War. Attention was now centered in the lower peninsula, some of it in the Park area, where the last of the undefeated and unremoved Seminoles had retreated into the Everglades. Moved by the old fear that the Indians might establish contact with sources of arms and ammunition outside of the United States, Fort Poinsett was reactivated, a new Fort Cross established at Palm Point or Middle Cape, and temporary military bases established on Chokoloskee Island and Pavilion Key.

In 1856 scouting officers reported that Indians had gathered corn from about an acre of ground on Chokoloskee Island. On the bank of the Pavionyhatchee or Chatham River they found a fertile field of twenty to forty acres. They reported that Indians had dug potatoes within the past three weeks, that some potatoes were still in the ground, and a few clumps of sugar cane were scattered over the fields. The soldiers found and destroyed about a dozen palmetto dwellings thought to have been occupied by four or five Indian families. Farther up the river they found an abandoned camp of fifteen or twenty rudely constructed palmetto shelters so new that the fronds used for thatching were still green.

Fort Cross became the base for a number of scouting expeditions in all directions early in 1857. According to records in the National Archives collected by Ray B. Seley of Miami, Fort Cross apparently became more important than the older Fort Poinsett. One may wonder whether the greater availability of fresh water there did not account for the shift of operations to Middle Cape.

Early in January, 1857, Captain I. P. McGown of the Fourth Artillery with a portion of his command in small boats scouted along the coast in the direction of the "Halbatahatchee River." A sketch map that accompanied the report shows that these scouts went eastward along the coast to about present day Flamingo, at which point a severe storm lasting forty-eight hours drove the boats southward to Ridgely's Key, approximately at the site of modern Joe Kemp Key. This report describes the area as belted by thick mangrove but the interior as prairie and hammock. Wells dug here and on other nearby keys failed to produce any water that was potable. Game was plentiful, but lack of fresh water forced the men to return to Fort Cross.

First Lieutenant H. H. Pelouse, scouting north and northwest from Fort Cross, ascended Little Sable Creek about twenty miles and guessed that it drained the lake northeast of Fort Cross (modern Lake Ingraham), which at that time had no outlet to the Gulf. The party fired the prairie as they moved upstream, and dug wells but always found the water brackish. Another party examining the region east and south of Fort Cross visited Arsnicker Keys, among others, on the way to Indian Key where they replenished their supply of drinking water, having been able to find none on the larger keys visited en route. On the return journey they found the keys in Florida Bay difficult to approach because of the shallow water. In March, Captain McGown left Fort Cross for a visit to Shark River and Whitewater Bay. He found an old Indian field about twelve miles from the head of the river and another at the entrance of the Everglades—likely at Avocado Mound.

Finally, in November, 1857, an expedition originated at Chokoloskee Island that for all practical purposes terminated the war. Captain John Parkhill led seventy five men up "Chokolisca" Creek, later named Turner River for Richard B. Turner, a guide. Nine miles up the river the party landed in the mangrove and marched three miles through the swamps to higher ground. After three days of scouting northward and westward they discovered and destroyed a large Indian settlement in a palm grove. On the following day they came upon two other Indian fields and destroyed them. Then tragedy struck when the desperate, hard-pressed Indians attacked while the soldiers were crossing a stream, killing Captain Parkhill, wounding five of his men, and ending the progress of the expedition.

The last hiding place of the Seminoles had been discovered, however, and further resistance was futile. Early in March of 1858 Chief Billy Bowlegs met with the opposition to negotiate the terms of removal. On May 8, 1858 Bowlegs and 123 of his followers, joined by forty-one others who had been captured, sailed for relocation in the West and the war was declared ended. The Seminoles remaining were not pursued further.

A by-product of the Seminole Wars appears in proposals for draining the Everglades. In 1848 Buckingham Smith, concluding that the principal military officers who had operated in the Everglades would know more about the interior than anyone else, addressed letters to them on the feasibility of such a project. In the replies there was general agreement that the hammocks were rich and should make good sugar plantations. General Thomas S. Jesup, whose stay in Florida had added little to his military laurels, responded that the swamps, if drained, would certainly grow olives, limes, and oranges. The officers were also interested in the problem of national security and recommended that the Florida Keys be fortified and a substantial populace be settled in the lower peninsula.

After the intense interest generated by the Seminole Wars, the southern Everglades attracted very little attention for some years. The activities of the War Between the States scarcely touched the region at all. In 1874 Edward King, who came south to report on reconstruction, contributed an article to *Scribner's Magazine* on Florida in which he predicted that a railroad would be built from Jacksonville to St. Augustine and down the east coast to Cape Sable, continuing on trestles to Key West, a project that was to be explored several times in the future.

Before any serious attention was given to building a railroad at least two expeditions penetrated the area to investigate the possibility of constructing a telegraph line to Cape Sable and on to Key West and Cuba. In 1870 one group examined the coastline while another evaluated the possibility of stringing the line across the Florida Keys on trees and across the intervening flats on poles. The vote was cast in favor of an underwater cable, as the overland plan was judged to be unfeasible because it would interfere too much with "the passage of the numerous sponge boats" and because of the difficult and wild nature of the terrain.

Some visitors to the area found the mangrove monotonous, but not Charles F. Holder, the author of *Along the Florida Reef*, in which he described the telegraph expedition. He wrote, "Nature seems to have varied the groupings of the mangrove in such a manner that new charms are presented at every remove." He thought it "a waste of nature's grandest exhibition to have these carnivals of splendid vegetation occurring in isolated places where it is but seldom they are seen."

In 1883 the *New Orleans Times Democrat* sponsored that newspaper's second Everglades exploring expedition. The first had viewed the Disston efforts at drainage in the Kissimmee River—Lake Okeechobee—Caloosahatchee complex and reported on the prospects for success and developments to follow. The second expedition was organized at Fort Myers and ascended the river to Lake Okeechobee preparatory to making the voyage from the lake down through the Everglades to Shark River. One object was to examine the possibility of a telegraph cable along that route. They began by probing the eight small rivers that entered the lake from the south in the hope of finding an all-water route to their destination. Most of the report is a description of the great effort required to hack their way through the sawgrass in the upper Glades. Having finally made their way to a point where they could use the boats they had been dragging along, they rapidly made their way to Shark River, reporting little of their impression of the lower Glades.

A few years later Daniel Hosea Bellou, a member of the expedition, wrote for *Harper's Weekly* (March 12, 1887) some rather highly imaginative impressions of the Glades that had not appeared in the official report. "Bird Life in the Everglades," he wrote, "is varied and interesting. Unfortunately the vast tribes of ducks, curlews and other edible birds never migrate. Thus they do not know what the sounds of firearms mean. They can be killed with a stick, and often taken in hand. It is unfortunate that they are satisfied with this secluded country. They fly but little, and their functions of flight are undergoing a process of degeneration. Their flesh is wormy, soft, and unfit to eat."

Camping in the Everglades, he reported, was full of discomforts and difficulties. Mosquitoes were ever present and worms by the million crawled over a daydreamer or sleeper. The trees offered shade and support for a hammock but were "inhabited with all manner of worms and insect life with and without legs, bugs, ticks, and other animals, minute in size but terrible in action, which drop wilfully and accidentally on the sleeper and promenade with great effect." The sounds of alligators and owls would have kept him awake anyhow, and leeches, he reported, were as numerous in the water as insects in the air.

Two manuscript accounts by travelers, Charles W. Pierce and Andrew Elliott Douglass, describing trips around the coast

Times Democrat Expedition in the Everglades

Birds feeding at headwaters of Shark River

by boat in the middle eighties, reveal the growing interest of naturalists in the region and throw new light on other activities. These trips could hardly be termed explorations as isolated settlers had established themselves here and there all along the coast.

In 1885, young Charles W. Pierce of Hypoluxo near Lake Worth engaged himself and his sloop, the *Bonton*, to escort naturalist, collector, and plume hunter and buyer Jean Chevelier on an expedition beginning at Miami and going by slow stages to Key West and up the west coast to Punta Gorda. Sailing with Pierce on the first leg of the journey from Hypoluxo to Miami were Guy Bradley, later a martyr to the cause of bird protection in the Park, and his brother Louis. The three youths made side trips to hunt along the way. Pierce's report revealed the great variety and quantity of wildlife on the "gold coast," Lake Worth to Miami, that would delight the custodians of any wildlife reservation.

From Barnes Sound, or maybe northeast Florida Bay, the Bradleys returned to Hypoluxo. Pierce had added William Wagner, son of a very early resident on the Miami River, to serve as man-of-all-work and cook, and Henry Wagner, a grandson, seventeen years old, enlisted as taxidermist to complete the crew. The term taxidermist may have been used somewhat loosely. Local residents recall that members of the Wagner family told how the "Old Frenchman," Chevelier, taught Henry how to mount birds for museum purposes. The entire crew was kept busy taking plumes from some of the birds for the feather market. At Lignum Vitae Key they met another collector sailing along in a small catboat. He reported that he was on the way to Cape Sable to collect crustacea for the Smithsonian Institution. There is reason to assume that this was Henry Hemphill, M.D., an amateur student of the crustacea who spent his vacations collecting for the United States National Museum for a number of years at about that time.

The *Bonton* and its crew called at East Cape and Palm Point. They sailed around Northwest Cape and entered Shark River, sailing upstream with the tide. The river with its wall of mangrove trees on either side impressed them tremendously. "The place looked wild and lonely. About three o'clock it seemed to get on Henry's nerves and we saw him crying, he would not tell us why, he was just plain scared," Pierce reported. On their way up the coast they visited John Gomez at Panther Key.

The same Henry Wagner also piloted Charles A. Dean and his daughter, Mrs. Eleanor H. D. Pearse, on a cruise from Miami around Cape Sable and up the west coast in the winter of 1895-1896. The cruise is described by Mrs. Pearse in her book *Florida's Vanishing Era.*

Andrew Elliott Douglass of New York made two excursions from St. Augustine to Key West and up the west coast in 1884 and 1885. He was primarily interested in examining Indian mounds along the coast. His expedition included a small crew for a limited amount of archaeological digging and study. He reported extensively on his findings and observations in unpublished letters to his wife. He touched only lightly in the area under study here, but such journeys make it obvious that travel around the area was becoming commonplace.

Nor was the interior neglected. Points of special interest were being discovered and rediscovered. Jack Jackson, a federal surveyor, ran the township lines in the Paradise Key area in 1847, but no publicity was given to his observation of the great stand of royal palms there. When in 1893 some Indians camping near Little River told of the unusual hammock with its royal palms, the Soar brothers, John and Marion, went to see it for themselves. They sailed to Black Point Creek, five miles south of Cutler, and went up the Creek to the edge of the pineland, followed the pineland southward until they sighted the palms, and walked and waded over to the hammock. Early in this century the stand of palms on Paradise Key was thought by many to be unique. Forgotten, if indeed ever generally known, was the royal palm hammock Andrew Canova had described when he visited the area of what is now southern Collier County during the Third Seminole War in the 1850's. Botanists were somewhat better informed, for Charles Torrey Simpson had visited the Collier County royal palms in the 1880's and other naturalists may have known about them. When the interior became better known it revealed other large stands of that magnificent tree.

The old surveyor's trail left by Jackson made overland travel to Paradise Key possible if slow, and an increasing number of scientists visited the spot. Another source of information about the interior comes from persons cruising along the Gulf Coast and Ten Thousand Islands. Kirk Munroe, who spent the winter of 1882 cruising on the west coast from Cedar Key to Key West, also probably visited Paradise Key. In February he made his headquarters at a camp of charcoal burners on Shark River. He had a medicine kit and successfully treated a suffering Negro at the camp. His reputation as a healer must have spread, for one day two Seminoles appeared in great haste to inquire if the white man would visit their camp in the Glades where a child was desperately ill. Munroe recalled that he had been taken almost due east from the headwaters of the river some twenty five or thirty miles to an Indian camp on the edge of a low hammock island or Everglades key on which many tall palms grew. The child had died before he arrived so he had no occasion to remain and explore. He evidently thought the presence of royal palms of no great significance at the time, but when they attracted so much attention later he surmised that it had been Paradise Key that he had visited. There is another hammock about ten miles west of Paradise Key in the pineland, but it was probably not used as an Indian camp. Park rangers who have surveyed the area from the air and other knowledgeable persons now generally agree that it must have been Paradise Key that Munroe visited.

The last extensive survey of the area was made in the winter of 1902–1903 by William J. Krome, locating and construction engineer for the Florida East Coast Railroad. He entered the Glades in November and came out in June. He surveyed the entire region from Florida City to Cape Sable to investigate the feasibility of building a railroad to Key West. His notes were lost or stolen, and he unfortunately never wrote an account of his experiences and observations.

The unusual archaeological find made by Frank Hamilton Cushing at Marco in 1896 inspired others to search for similar evidence of the extensive Indian culture on the lower Gulf coast. Clarence B. Moore was the most active of these, making annual trips until 1926 when a hurricane destroyed the *Gopher*, a small steamer he used on the expeditions and after which Gopher Key is named.

The area could no longer be considered unexplored. Early in this century reports about the entire region began to have wide circulation. A. W. and Julian A. Dimock made several extensive trips through the interior, collecting zoological specimens, taking many excellent photographs, and writing a very popular book about its places and people.

By 1909 when another edition was published of Hugh L. Willoughby's "rather hair-raising story" about a canoe trip across the southern Everglades (*Across the Everglades,* first published in 1898), Commodore Ralph M. Munroe of Coconut Grove expressed himself in a letter to a friend as being completely unimpressed. Hundreds of sports and market hunters, he said, were at home there. At about the same time A. W. Dimock wrote that in crossing the Everglades in a boat one might meet delay but not danger; that it was not an adventure but a picnic.

Feather hunters had long since made their way to every important rookery. Other hunters and trappers had scoured the region in their search for game and had begun to complain about the comparative scarcity of wildlife of all kinds. The road to Paradise Key built in 1915 and its extension to Flamingo in 1922 opened the Park area to more extensive exploration and exploitation of its natural wealth, and the completion of the Tamiami Trail in 1928 also made penetration easier. Collectors of rare fauna and flora soon visited and revisited every hammock in the Everglades.

In 1917 a small surveying expedition was reported lost in the region. John King and his son, John, and William Catlow, Jr. left Miami in a glades skiff to look over some of the lands of the Chevelier Company. It was February and the time of low water in the Everglades. They meant to follow a course just south of the Tamiami Trail, then under construction, but had to move farther southward to find enough water to float the skiff. They soon realized that they should follow such small streams as they could find and make their way to one of the Gulf coast rivers. As they did this their stock of food ran low. It was so dry that game had left the area and they were about to be reduced to a diet of garfish and palm hearts when they reached the Shark River. A fisherman conducted them to the bark factory near the mouth of the river, where they caught the next boat carrying tanbark to Key West, stopping en route to take on a cargo of coconuts at Cape Sable. They finally made their way home, never really having been hopelessly lost.

The once-isolated land was being penetrated, and by the early 1920's the curious and adventurous as well as profiteers and vandals roamed almost at will throughout the Everglades.

MAP BY J. FLOYD MONK

CHOKOLOSKEE BAY
Halfway Cr.
CHOKOLOSKEE
Turner Riv.
SUNDAY BAY
OYSTER BAY
Lopez Riv.
TURTLE KEY
Huston Riv.
RABBIT KEY
CHEVELIER BAY
WATSON PLACE
LITTLE PAVILION KEY
Chatham Riv.
POSSUM KEY
CANNON BAY
PAVILION KEY
DUCK ROCK
CHATHAM BEND
MORMON KEY
GOPHER KEY
ALLIGATOR BAY
CANAL
CLAM PT.
MOSQUITO KEY
BUZZARD KEY
SNAKE KEY
TURKEY KEY
Two Island Bay
SEMINOLE POINT
PLOVER KEY
ONION KEY
Onion Key Bay
ALLIGATOR COVE
ALLIGATOR PT.
BIRD KEY
WOOD KEY
PORPOISE PT.
SECOND BAY
HOG KEY
CANAL
FIRST BAY
Lostman's Riv.
G U L F   O F   M E X I C O
JOHNSON HAMMOCK
HIGHLAND PT.
Rodgers Riv.
HIGHLAND Big Creek
HIGHLAND BEACH
Broad Riv.

0   1   2   3   4   5   6
NAUTICAL MILES

IV Chatham Bend and Possum Key

SIGNS OF HUMAN OCCUPATION exist on almost every habitable bit of land on the western side of the Park, but the evidence is rapidly disappearing as nature reasserts control over abandoned homesites and fields. Here and there exotic plants and trees betray the hand of man who planted them, and a further search is likely to turn up bits of metal, crockery, or glass—and maybe the remains of a cistern. Hurricane Donna in September, 1960 uncovered forgotten trails and clearings that stood out distinctly after the storm, temporarily uncovered from the encroaching wilderness. These former homesites range from tiny beaches and keys that accommodated a home or two to a forty-acre tract at Chatham Bend. More often than not, small or large, they were associated with shell heaps left by Calusa Indians.

The Ten Thousand Islands and mangrove coast area was little known to white men until the end of the last century. In 1885, after a cruise on that coast, one visitor said of maps of the area, "for general outline they were superb, but for particulars all of them were signal failures. As we worked further south they were quite useless." He also called it "not a populous shore" with less than three hundred souls from Punta Rassa to Cape Sable. He occasionally saw a Nassau sponger with her colored crew, sometimes a Gulf steamer, and three or four times small boats came out of passes with a few bushels of vegetables for Key West. Curiously enough, he turned back at Pavilion Key, writing off the coast from there to Cape Sable as not interesting.

Dozens of persons who once lived in this area can still be located to tell their stories of how they lived, often perched precariously on patches of land scarcely above normal high tides. This Florida frontier attracted and bred a particularly hardy type of men and women. They lived in such isolation

Chatham River and Possum Key

that they were compelled to be self-sufficient and, indeed, it was precisely this isolation that attracted some people. Their only contact with each other and the outside world was by boat—in the early days a skiff propelled by oars, or perhaps a sailboat. They lived at the mercy of storms and high water, building and rebuilding homes they knew would likely one day be destroyed.

They lived on the bounty of nature as generous in some ways as it was harsh in others. Soil was scarce but what there was of it was fertile. The settlers farmed to a limited extent both for food and for market. Commercial fishing was the mainstay of the economy, but hunting animals and birds for their skins and feathers was at times more important. Wood cutting and charcoal making added a small but sure means of livelihood. Some people operated small boats that carried away the products of the region and brought back supplies. Their lives were undoubtedly far more varied, certainly more independent, and quite possibly more materially and spiritually rewarding than that of some of their descendants who still live in scattered areas on the western coast.

Every frontier has its lawless elements, and legends about the early days of this area have become more lurid over the years. From many popular notions one might believe that it was peopled principally by outlaws, murderers, and such. But while it had its share of refugees from law and order, they by no means made up the majority of its early inhabitants.

An extreme example of legend making concerning the western Park area appeared in London's *Blackwood's Magazine* in a 1927 article entitled "The Ten Thousand Islands" under the name of Major L. A. M. Jones. The following paragraphs are quoted from that source.

> The first settlers in the Ten Thousand Islands are believed to have been a Scotsman, his wife, and two daughters, and an Englishman, who were shipwrecked on their way back from Virginia over a hundred years ago. Their inbred progeny exists to-day on one of the biggest of the northernmost isles as a tribe of giant white men, whose minds are the dwarfed minds of six-year-old children, and who have five fingers and five toes instead of

four. I believe that the females of this idiot colony are practically the only women in this queer corner of the world.

But those who may be described as the "real" inhabitants of the islands are not idiots. Far from it! Hidden, each in his own island, are Robinson Crusoes and Alexander Selkirks by the score, nearly every one of whom is a dangerous outlaw. In the Ten Thousand Islands there are men whose lives of crime and adventure are equal in enthralling interest to anything that the imagination of Joseph Conrad ever invented. Silent, bearded, and unkempt, they do not loiter, and they never talk. Their sole costume consists of an old shirt and tattered trousers, in the hip pocket of which can be plainly seen the outline of a heavy Colt—nothing more. Shoes are not known.

The islands, of which comparatively few are inhabited, are separated from each other by a system of tortuous and shallow channels, which are more confusing than any maze. Only an Islander can find his way through them, and as each man discreetly confines himself to the immediate neighborhood of his own particular island, there is probably not a single inhabitant to whom all the channels are known. The U.S. Government once put up signposts to mark a channel for yachts. The Islanders quickly rendered them useless by turning them in all directions but the right one.

The arrival of another fugitive from justice in these mournful solitudes soon spreads around in some mysterious way; but many will be the moons that must wax and wane, and long and close indeed the scrutiny of the newcomer and his movements from afar off, before any sign is given that his fellow exiles are aware even of his existence.

The Sheriffs and Deputy Sheriffs of the various counties in whose jurisdiction the islands lie will not land there to serve a warrant on an Islander. Too many Sheriffs and Deputy Sheriffs have been killed in doing so. Incidentally, no Islander has so far been induced to become an officer of the law, nor has there ever been a case of one of them betraying a fellow-Islander. Truly an example of "honour among thieves."

In this little world of crooks and human derelicts, every one is known by a "nickname," such as "The Kink Fisher," "The Shark Killer," (there are many sharks in these waters), or "The Sailor," and so on.

They have seven unwritten laws, outside the observance of

which all other laws, religious or moral systems are anathema to them. They are:—

Suspect every man.
Ask no questions.
Settle your own quarrels.
Never steal from an Islander.
Stick by him, even if you do not know him.
Shoot quick, when your secret is in danger.
Cover your kill.

A check against established historical facts sometimes serves to measure the degree of exaggeration. The Audubon Society lost one warden sent into the area to protect the plume birds. But in this version "Four of them were murdered, and their bodies found covered with the skins of egrets they had come to protect. The fifth told the story in a hospital ward when recovering from his wounds." Equally distorted but curiously interesting for the kernel of truth is the following.

> To describe the fauna of the islands is a very simple matter. The coco-nut tree furnishes the Islander with house, house furniture, clothing, table utensil, food, and drink. Panther, cabbage-bears, Florida beaver, and a very small species of deer provide him with his winter hunting, though there is little money to be made from it, as the pelts are very poor owing to the climate. The only exception to this rule is to be found in the case of the raccoons, whose fur is of exceptionally good quality, and forms 90 per cent of the island's small pelt trade.

Perhaps the story of Edward J. "Ed" Watson best illustrates the survival and growth of the worst elements in such a frontier story, as he appears to have been a strange combination of the best and worst qualities of such men. Though he came to a tragic and violent end half a century ago, Ed Watson is by all odds the "best known" of all white men who ever lived in the western Park area. He was unusually successful at wresting a life from the wilderness, and while others lived at Chatham Bend before and after him, his land is still known as the "Watson Place."

Watson established himself on a forty-acre shell mound near the mouth of the Chatham River in the 1890's and became a highly successful farmer, growing sugar cane and making syrup

The Watson Place on Chatham River

on a large scale as well as producing vegetables for the Key West–New York market. He built a substantial two story house that was kept painted and in good repair, in sharp contrast to the palmetto thatch and unpainted board buildings commonly seen in the area. Nearby on the river front he owned another building with quarters for workmen, boat storage, and workshop area.

Part of the Watson house stood until it was razed after being damaged by Hurricane Donna in 1960. An old syrup kettle set in a brick furnace still remains in good condition. Part of the steam boiler used to provide power for the cane mill and to cook the juice to make syrup or sugar also remains on the site. Concrete pillars mark the locations of all buildings, and the National Park Service has plans for a camping ground on the spot.

But Watson is best remembered today as the bad man of that coast. Even people who knew him personally tell conflicting stories. What appears here may be yet another version of the story, but it at least has the virtue of being based on accounts of people who actually knew him. His contemporaries agree that he was generous, kind hearted, friendly, and ready to do a favor, and also that he had a fearful temper when aroused. Not one of them accuses him of having done them any wrong of any sort.

Watson employed many men and some women, of whom some were his friends and neighbors. Others were undoubtedly refugees from the law to whom Watson offered employment and temporary security with no questions asked. Others were probably drifters who stayed a while and then went on their way. Perhaps only an Ed Watson could have made a usable labor force of such dubious elements.

The fearsome reputation Watson acquired in his own day has grown with the passage of time. He had maintained friendly relations with most of his neighbors, but they became more and more afraid of him and in the end this was his undoing. The only neighbor with whom he had actually had an altercation had left the area ten years before Watson met his violent end.

Watson came from a respectable central Florida family. His marriages seemed successful. All of his sons and daughters had good reputations and none seemed to have inherited their father's penchant for trouble. One is forced to conclude that Watson told some of the stories that built his bad reputation— that, purposefully or not, he himself helped create the Watson legend.

Two persons who knew him well are among those who have related the Watson story. Charles S. "Ted" Smallwood, who kept a store and served as postmaster at Chokoloskee, traded with him and was known as his friend. It may be that Watson supplied much of the data that appeared in Smallwood's reminiscences published in 1955. Another friend was James Henry Thompson, who lived with Watson when he was a teenage boy for five years between 1892 and 1897. Thompson comments that often when they were alone and there was nothing to do on long evenings that Watson would talk about his past. Thompson remained on good terms with Watson and later returned to his employ for some four years, operating Watson's boats from Key West to Tampa.

The Smallwood and Thompson stories are in agreement only about the events in the Ten Thousand Island phases of his life. Watson's troubles seem to have started early when he shot a Negro, reportedly because he feared the Negro would tell his father about his carelessness in pea planting. He rode away to Texas (or Arkansas, according to other sources) where he became associated with the family of Belle Starr, the notorious outlaw and ex-spy. The Starrs were interested in a piece of property which he and Belle rode out to see. According to one version, Watson had a premonition that Belle's family was "about to do him in" so he shot her and fled. Another version says he paid her some money for a piece of land and later waylaid her, killed her, and "recovered" his money. Another suggests he killed her for "two-timing" him. A more plausible story is that Belle Starr was killed by a member of her own unscrupulous family.

At any rate, Watson had to move on, and he went to Oregon where he was married and fathered four children, three boys and a girl, before he got into trouble again. Someone there put a shotgun blast, which went harmlessly over his bed, through his bedroom window. He apparently knew whom to suspect, for he sought his attacker out the next morning, shot him, and fled to Florida, leaving his family behind. There, in Arcadia, he came across "another bad actor," Quinn Bass, who was beating a smaller man. When Watson admonished Bass to stop, Bass turned on Watson, who then killed Bass in self-defense.

By this chain of circumstances Watson came to Half Way Creek about 1892 or 1893 with a previous reputation for violence scattered in widely separated places. He first worked for local truck farmers, but soon acquired an old schooner, cut buttonwood, and freighted wood to Key West. When a man named Will Raymond who lived at Chatham Bend was killed in a brush with the law in Key West, Watson purchased his claim and launched his highly successful farming enterprise.

His first trouble at Chatham Bend was with Adolphus Santini of Chokoloskee, whom he "cut" seriously in the neck during an argument in a Key West auction room; this scrape reportedly cost Watson a large sum of money to settle. In the course of the investigation of the knifing, authorities backtracked Watson to Oregon to see if he was wanted there. By this chance his wife discovered Watson's whereabouts. He sent money for her to come with the children to Chokoloskee, where she died a year later.

Watson's reputation made him a ready suspect. He reportedly bought a claim on Lostman's River and when a squatter and his nephew living there refused to move away and were killed, "they laid it on Watson." Watson's son Robert ran away to Key West, sold the schooner, and returned to Oregon. A man named Collins reportedly gave Watson false information about his son, and Watson attacked Collins. He bought a farm in Columbia County in north central Florida and when two troublemakers there were killed people again "laid it on Watson." It is not surprising that fearful rumors began to circulate about the troubles at Chatham Bend and that even local residents from nearby settlements avoided Watson's area.

In 1910 a worse than usual collection of outlanders came to the Watson Place. Among them was Leslie Cox, who came from farther up the coast, and Duchy Melvin from Key West, who had "killed a policeman and burned a factory or two." Hannah Smith, a man named Waller, and an unnamed Negro completed the group. Ted Smallwood recounted part of the story. "I thought something would soon happen and it did. Watson came up here one day; brought Duchy, left Cox, Hannah and Waller down there and the nigger. The nigger said they killed Hannah and Waller while Watson was up here and when Watson and Duchy went back that night they killed Duchy and put him in the Creek."

A man named Cannon who had a claim farther inland at Possum Key discovered Hannah Smith's body in the shallow waters of the river while going downriver with a crew of men to dig clams. The men buried the woman's body and alerted the community. Watson left for Fort Myers to bring the sheriff down to arrest Cox for the murders, but the October 17, 1910 hurricane intervened and the sheriff turned back at Marco. Taking the law into his own hands, Watson bought some storm-wet gun shells and set out from Smallwood's store to hunt Cox. He returned in a few days with a hat that he said belonged to Cox, and reported that he had killed Cox.

The crowd that had gathered at the dock was not satisfied with the story and wanted to see Cox's body for proof. Some of the men agreed to return to Chatham Bend with Watson to see the body. Then the question was raised as to whether or not Watson should be allowed to carry his gun. This or something else angered him. Before anyone in the startled crowd could move into action, Watson is said to have raised his gun, snapped both barrels on the wet shells, which failed to fire, and started to reach for his sixshooter. By common consent it is agreed that Luke Short, a Negro who was standing somewhat apart, fired first at Watson. A fusilade of shots from the others followed, and Watson was killed. His neighbors buried him on nearby Rabbit Key, but his body was moved a few days later and buried at Fort Myers where his wife's family lived.

The sheriff came down to investigate the shooting, and the men who had been present were summoned to Fort Myers to testify at a hearing. Nothing was ever done to establish fact or responsibility for the shooting, leaving many unanswered questions and more fodder for the Watson legend. When asked fifty years later why Watson's neighbors had shot him, an on-looker explained simply, "They were scared."

Watson may have been a victim of his own violent temper, and his growing reputation for violence. Whether he was really guilty of all the fearsome things charged to him or whether the oft-repeated stories frightened those at hand into hasty and unwise action will never be surely known.

With Watson dead, his neighbors were even more frightened because they fully expected Cox and other desperados to descend upon them at any moment. The fear that Cox was not dead persisted. C. G. McKinney of Chokoloskee voiced that fear when he wrote in his newspaper column on December 1, 1910, "We hear a rumor that Mr. Leslie Cox is still living and ready for business at any moment." Four weeks later, McKinney wrote, "We have nothing definite from Mr. Cox yet. He will turn up soon I think." And on January 5, McKinney reported the rumor that Cox had gone to Georgia. If he had not been killed, he certainly disappeared. In a letter to this writer in 1955 his sister reported that the family had never heard from him again after the 1910 episode.

The Watson Place was never farmed much after Watson's death, and none of his descendants ever lived there. The Chevelier Corporation, named for Jean Chevelier, as was Chevelier Bay, acquired the Watson property in 1919, and planned

drainage and development of part of it. In 1920 the corporation employed Erben Cook of Miami to survey it in an effort to
locate their property lines. Cook established headquarters at
the Watson Place and spent much time there in the next two
years. Since the Tamiami Trail was not yet open he would
travel from Miami to Flamingo by going down the newly constructed road by automobile or truck instead of sailing around
Cape Sable. Cook built a dock on the shore of Coot Bay, and
traveled the shorter and safer inland route by boat through
Whitewater Bay and Shark River out to the Gulf of Mexico
and up the coast to Chatham River. He could also go up Broad
River and make his way by inland passage, a much longer but
safer journey in rough weather.

Cook and his associates were remarkably successful at finding the corner posts marking the old property lines. The federal
suveyor's notes were good and frequently it was possible to
find the rotted underground portion of the forty-year-old
stakes. The surveyor in addition had blazed nearby trees, indicating their relation to the true corners of the lines and
cutting identifying numbers in the blazed surfaces.

When they were unsuccessful at locating a township or section line, Cook called upon "Uncle Billy" Roberts, who had
uncanny skill at finding the markers. Then a man of seventy,
Uncle Billy had hunted over the area when the blazes were
fresher and could often recall just where the line could be
found. He was not bothered by the mosquitoes that made life
almost unbearable for the others in the group. His associates
attributed his immunity to his habit of eating a half plug of
Brown's Mule chewing tobacco each morning, thereby producing what might be called the "Original Black Leaf 40 Insect
Killer."

Once the surveyors came across a moonshiner with his still
set up on the marl prairie where it could easily be seen by
anyone going upriver. Asked if he was not afraid of being
discovered, the moonshiner replied that he had to risk it because the mosquitoes were too bad back in the woods. The
likelihood that anyone would bother him if he were discovered
seems remote.

Without benefit of engineering advice the Chevelier Com-

pany cut a few ill-advised drainage canals in areas where the
water level proved to be controlled either by the waters of the
ocean or of the Everglades, depending on the volume of fresh
water in the interior. Drainage ditches turned into tidal
streams, letting in as much water as was let out. The company
kept caretakers at the Watson Place until 1929 when the development plans had to be abandoned, as were so many other
of Florida's boom-time dreams. The final use of the Watson
Place before it became a part of Everglades National Park was
its role as a weekend camp of some Miamians, who used it
as a base for fishing and hunting expeditions.

Possum Key has seven or eight acres of land and a history
of almost continuous occupation since the 1880's. It is tucked
away in the maze of islands some eighteen miles southeast of
the town of Everglades. Its relatively high elevation, fertile soil,
and its location on a deep channel protected from Gulf
storms by a fringe of mangrove islands account for its importance. It acquired the name "Chevelier Place" when Jean
Chevelier established himself there late in the 1880's. The
Coast and Geodetic Survey Map of 1889 shows the site and
also the one on Chatham Bend, shortly to be known as the
Watson Place, as the "Raymond Place."

Chevelier apparently knew both coasts of the lower peninsula rather well. He knew where to put in for water in the
Florida Keys–Florida Bay region, and was familiar with the
channel into Key West prior to chartering the *Bonton* for a
cruise in 1885. He was known variously as a naturalist, a taxidermist, and a collector of bird specimens for museums. He was
known as being something of an eccentric, and was often referred to as "the old Frenchman." William B. Robertson, Jr., a
National Park Service biologist, made an extensive search for
information on Chevelier's Florida activities when writing
ornithological notes for "The Cruise of the *Bonton*," by
Charles W. Pierce, recently published. Dr. Robertson concludes
that Chevelier may have been the first large-scale plume hunter and buyer to operate on the Gulf coast. It also appears that
he may have been a scientific collector of considerable importance. Evidence in the Pierce narrative supports either interpre-
tation of his activities. The party on the *Bonton* concentrated

upon birds of greatest demand for the feather trade. The sale of plumes seems to have been the way the cruise was financed. However, the careful method of preparing the skins and the number of birds taken of little or no feather value suggests they were collected for scientific purposes. Dr. Robertson suspects that Chevelier sent specimens of Florida birds to museums and collectors in Europe, many of which later found their way back into museums in this country.

How and when Chevelier discovered Possum Key and chanced to locate there is not known. He was not the only person to live there, nor was he the only resident at the time of his stay. Lige Carey of Key West built a two-story house where the cistern now stands. Chevelier's smaller house was around the corner to the east some fifty yards away. The large house remained there after Chevelier's was dismantled and moved away. Some think that Chevelier induced Carey to build there to establish a base for plume hunting and trading. Chevelier could scarcely have found enough jobs in taxidermy to justify his stay, and must have combined the preparation of museum specimens with the feather trade.

James Henry Thompson when in his early teens spent a year with Chevelier. Thompson recalls that Chevelier selected one of three guns of different fire power to avoid ruining the specimens he shot, and that he required the skins and feathers to be prepared more carefully than other traders. Chevelier stayed on Possum Key but was primarily interested in nearby Gopher Key, which he considered his own special property. C. T. Boggess, another "old timer," recalls a twelve by twelve foot house on Gopher Key, very likely a palmetto thatched shack.

Chevelier was thought to have money, and the suspicion developed that he had buried it on Gopher Key. Indeed, the notion seems to persist. In 1961 Park rangers found an elaborate metal detector appraised at $350 on the key. They confiscated it, along with complete camping equipment also found, and waited for a claimant. One finally came forward and recovered all of his property except for the metal detector. He was given a suspended fine and a warning not to explore any further. Gopher Key is also of interest to archaeologists who will very likely sometime excavate parts of an Indian burial ground there. About 1894 a French family with two daughters, the Courlys, came to live with Chevelier. They brought a piano and other items of civilization unusual to this watery island wilderness. Their names appear frequently in the diary of Adolphus Santini on Chokoloskee Island, who reported exchanges of visits between the two families. After Chevelier died in 1895 the Courlys moved their house to Pavilion Key for a time. On May 9, Santini reported that two members of his family were helping to put up Courly's house on Pavilion Key. On July 8 "They moved the piano to Pavilion Key." They later again dismantled the dwelling and moved it to Buena Vista (now Miami), where it became part of a hotel structure at 36th Street and N. E. Second Avenue. According to local sources, Dick Sawyer stopped at Pavilion Key for a few days to pull his boat from the water and scrape its bottom. He told the Courlys about Miami and they loaded all their possessions on his boat and sailed there with him.

Meanwhile, stories of the Chevelier treasure did not die even though the family, some reports said, lived in poverty and "nearly starved to death" on the island. In true romantic fashion, one story said that a local swain of one of the Courly girls killed the old Frenchman when he would not reveal the hiding place of the money, and then dug up the entire island in a frantic search for it. In another version Chevelier is said to have disliked the courtship of his "niece" (she was actually unrelated) and moved away to break up the romance.

Leon Hamilton and his sister Mary considered themselves godchildren of Chevelier and, presumably before the Courlys appeared on the scene, had been promised that they were to be Chevelier's heirs. Leon remembers that as a lad of nine or ten years he and his sister were summoned to the bedside of the dying man. But if Chevelier had meant to tell them where the treasure lay buried it was too late, for he had already lost the power of coherent speech.

Bill House of Chokoloskee was also associated with Chevelier. Among his activities was gathering swallow-tailed kite eggs for collectors. He explained years later to a visitor who engaged his charter boat that he had worked as a guide and

assistant to a Frenchman who gave him addresses of buyers
so he could carry on the work. House then acted as a "broker"
for his neighbors, buying eggs they found and reselling them.
The prices ranged from $7.50 to $15.00 per egg—depending
on how well marked they were.

The Dimocks, in relating the story of their trip which started
at Everglades in 1907, reported they had camped on Possum
Key. The big Carey house was padlocked but they pitched tents
on the island and helped themselves to avocado pears, bananas, sugar cane, sweet potatoes, and guavas. They later also
stopped at Onion Key on Lostman's River but reported no
activity there. Old timers remember a man known only as
Mr. James who worked for short periods of time for George
W. Storter, Jr. at Everglades and who, as soon as he accumulat-
ed a small grubstake, went to stay a while at Possum Key.
Oddly enough, nobody suggests that he was seeking Chevelier's
treasure. Hunters and fishermen recall camping there frequently
but none can explain how or when the house was moved or
destroyed.

The story of Possum Key after the death of Chevelier is
somewhat sketchy as to details of names, dates, or occupations
of other residents. One photograph (unfortunately undated)
shows only a poinciana tree and the cistern to mark the site
of the big house. Of the succession of people who lived there,
however, none is more interesting than the last, who is still
there in 1967.

Arthur Leslie Darwin, the present occupant of Possum Key,
has the distinction of being the last private resident on Park
lands. His squatter's rights were so well established and his
opposition to moving so great that he has been allowed to remain. He claims fifth generation descent from the famous
scientist Charles Darwin. Born in Arkansas, Arthur was living
in Texas with his wife and nine children when he took to
the Gulf waters in 1934 to avoid taking a WPA job. He and
a companion worked their way around to Key West, trying
vainly to break into the depression-ridden commercial fishing
business. He started his life in the Park area at Gene Hamilton's place on Lostman's River. He became a trapper there
in 1935, catching thirty five otters on Broad River and ten

times as many raccoons. This he continued for eight years, turning to alligator hunting in summer. In 1942 he went to Chokoloskee and Everglades, working in boat yards as a carpenter until he finally retired to Possum Key in 1945.

Starting out with only a tent, he before long brought in cement from Everglades, shell from nearby sources, and sand from Pavilion Key, and made his own concrete blocks for the small house he still uses. He put out 350 banana plants, which have sometimes suffered from salt water intrusion into the soil in dry weather and occasionally from frost, but which at this writing still stand. Apple bananas sell best, he reports, but the

Arthur Leslie Darwin at Possum Key

horse banana is sturdier and will take more salt. His best cus-
tomers are people along the coast accustomed to and preferring
the taste of the local bananas. Darwin has fished and hunted
at times, and built a few boats, but he is now retired on an
old age pension. Over the years he has killed twenty six rattle-
snakes on Possum Key. None have been seen in recent years;
the last known one was found by a Park ranger in 1961.

Many boats pass Darwin's way now, but he saw very few
in the early days. Boaters often get lost and he shows them the
way out. He cooks with gas, heats with a kerosene stove, and
uses a kerosene lamp but keeps a battery-powered headlight
for hunting. Panthers and other animals come to his cistern for
fresh water. A board in the cistern permits them to climb out
and avoid drowning in his drinking water. This is a wise
precaution—many wild animals have been trapped in abandoned cisterns which they enter in search of water only to
find it impossible to scale the smooth walls afterward. Panthers
are rare, but Darwin recently complained that bears were eating
his bananas. Darwin, at seventy-eight years of age in 1967,
wishes he were younger so that he might go to Honduras where
he hears it is not so populated as the Ten Thousand Islands.

Another hermit who lives closer to civilization without becoming involved with it is Robert Roy Osmer. He was a sea-
man during World War I on a boat that was decommissioned
at Jacksonville, Florida. Instead of returning home to Decatur,
Georgia, his birthplace, he went to Everglades after seeing an
advertisement of the Barron Collier Company for workers in
their development. He remained there until 1927 when he went
to North Carolina for a time as a ranger in the Nantahala
and Mt. Pisgah national forests. He remained in Tennessee
and spent some years trying his hand at farming, storekeeping,
and running a local newspaper. After another stint in the
merchant marine in World War II, he came back to South
Florida and in February, 1949, settled himself on Pelican Key
just off the channel from the Gulf of Mexico to Everglades.
Pelican Key has now been renamed Comer Key at the request
of the National Park Service, after a former governor of Alabama who used to camp there with his family.

Osmer built a shack for himself and collected numerous

objects representative of the area and a library of several hundred volumes. A relatively well educated man, he received many visitors when weather permitted. He served coffee and philosophy to all comers, many of whom brought him food or money. Had he wished to get entirely away from people he certainly would have been compelled to leave Pelican Key.

Hurricane Donna swept away Osmer's shack and nearly all of the vegetation on the key, ending his stay there. Park authorities had agreed to let him remain as long as he wished unless some such disaster occurred. Osmer spent a short time in Tennessee after the hurricane, but returned to Everglades to seek another island retreat. He finally selected Gomez Key just outside of Park boundaries. But the new site had disadvantages as it lies off the beaten path and he received fewer visitors, though many of his old friends still called regularly. There was no deep channel close inshore there as there was at Pelican Key. Osmer for a time wrote a column for the *Collier County News* that he called "Adventures in Solitude." He subsequently left Gomez Key and lived on a houseboat which he beached nearby at small White Horse Key where passing or visiting boats could more easily come alongside. Early in 1967 he retired from island living to Ochopee, where he now lives in a trailer.

Hurricane Donna ended the occupation of many other sites in the same way, and swept away the remains of long abandoned buildings in other cases. Three fishing shacks on Turkey Key were blown away and, because of Park regulations, could not be replaced. Two old houses that stood on Mormon Key, mute evidence of an earlier era, also disappeared in the great storm.

Commercial fishermen still rendezvoused in the Turkey Key area for a time, some living on houseboats. Runboats brought them supplies and took away their catch. The runboat service then became irregular and finally ceased, and the fishermen now live in Chokoloskee or Everglades, boating to the region to fish and delivering their catch to their local fishhouses on their return.

Panther, or Gomez Key, is historically famous as the home of John Gomez, one of the most colorful characters in the early history of the area. He called himself a farmer in the census of 1880 and he and Captain Horr, of Horr's Island near Marco, reportedly attempted to raise goats. These were all eaten by panthers—hence the name of the key. Passersby reported visiting Gomez and his wife there in 1885, finding them deliriously happy to have visitors. Charles W. Pierce, one of the visitors, recalled having met Gomez and his "cracker wife" at Cedar Key thirteen years earlier. They lived on the exposed side of the island, perhaps to see any passing boats. Later residents all lived on the other side, away from the Gulf of Mexico.

In 1898 Kenneth Ransom of St. Joseph, Michigan and three youthful companions paid a visit to Panther Key. The lads had sailed down the Mississippi and were on their way around the Gulf coast to the Atlantic, planning to make their way back home by way of the Erie Canal and the Great Lakes. By

John Gomez, wife, and home, Panther Key, 1898

sheer chance they put in at Panther Key in search of water, the one place in the region where it could be found. They also found Gomez, who told them he would be 123 years of age at the end of that year. They described his wife as a young woman, but of him they wrote, "his complexion was brown, dark and rich [in] color as century old mahogany; his thick white hair, bushy and plentiful, framed a face seamed and lined but keen and full of vigor." They also left an excellent photograph of the Gomez cabin, a two room palmetto thatch structure that local sources say was built by two plume buyers named Pinicker and Brown and later given to him. The boys cruised in the islands for a week without seeing another white man. Their adventures are described in *A Year in a Yawl,* by Russell Doubleday.

By his own account, Gomez was born in 1778 (which would have made him only 120 years old when the Michigan boys visited him), served with Napoleon Bonaparte, was cabin boy for the pirate Gasparilla, took part in the Battle of Okeechobee in the Seminole War in 1837, was a slaver and blockade runner in the Civil War, and spoke seven languages. Local residents remembered him only as a very old man who wore a heavy white beard. Old John was found drowned in July, 1900. Others have occupied the key from time to time, but none have dimmed the romantic story he left the key.

Panther Key was visited regularly for the fresh water there, and James Henry Thompson, among others, once lived there. For four years he used it as a base for the operating freight boats between Key West and Tampa for Ed Watson. It was conveniently located for an overnight stop while traveling in either direction.

Joe Dickman, born about 1880, came to the region at about age 50, and thirty five years later *Miami Herald* columnist Steve Trumbull pronounced him a "bona fide recluse" and dubbed him "hermit emeritus" when he retired from Cape Romano where he had lived most of the time. Eardly Foster Atkinson came to Dismal Key in the early 1950's. In the July 18, 1963 edition of the *Collier County News* Roy Ozmer reported that he had had the other three hermits as guests at his "hermitage" on Gomez Key.

Even outside of Park boundaries the islands are seldom occupied nowadays except for short times by campers, hunters, and fishermen. Nearby Fakahatchee Island is much larger and higher, and was long occupied by several families. It had enough people early in the century to maintain a school. Now only abandoned buildings mark its former importance.

Sandfly Island on the south side of Chokoloskee Bay was once the scene of tomato planting, a packing shed, and a small store kept by Joe Wiggins. Barron Collier thought well enough of its promise for development to drill a well in which he found potable, if somewhat brackish water—a rarity in the area and only found elsewhere nearby on Chokoloskee Island.

The creation of the Park with boundaries that reach into Chokoloskee Bay means that the entire region will revert to and remain in a state of nature. Visitors will seldom realize that well into the twentieth century a number of colorful people called this area home.

V   On Lostman's and Shark River

EXCEPT FOR THE GREATER ISOLATION of the more southerly settlements on the mangrove coast and the fact that the Ten Thousand Islands were a less prominent feature of the landscape, many of the same conditions of life prevailed in the lower part of the western Park area as in the upper regions. They are not distinctly different sections, but the two major rivers in the southern portion—Lostman's and Shark—are the best known geographical features, as were Chatham Bend and Possum Key in the upper area.

Many of the same people lived at one time or another in both areas, but a few individuals or families became closely identified with each. Lostman's River, for instance, was peculiarly the province of people named Hamilton, many of them not related to one another. Hamiltons were not the first or only people there, but they remained long after others had departed.

Lostman's River is sometimes called Lossman's or Lawsman's River; differences in spelling arise from conflicting stories about the origin of the name. One theory is that it was meant to mark a significant proper name. David Graham Copeland thought it might be a corruption of Lawson's from the surgeon general by that name who led the reconnaissance expedition there in the Seminole Wars.

Several other versions suggest it may have been named after a lost man or lost men. One story tells of five soldiers at Key West who hired a Captain Jocelyn to take them up the coast to Punta Rassa. Though they were in civilian clothes the captain suspected them of being deserters because they hid in the hold of his sloop. He put them off at the river and told them about a sawmill back in the woods where they might hide and work. Another story tends to confirm this. William Smith Allen while en route to Key West saw someone waving a white cloth from

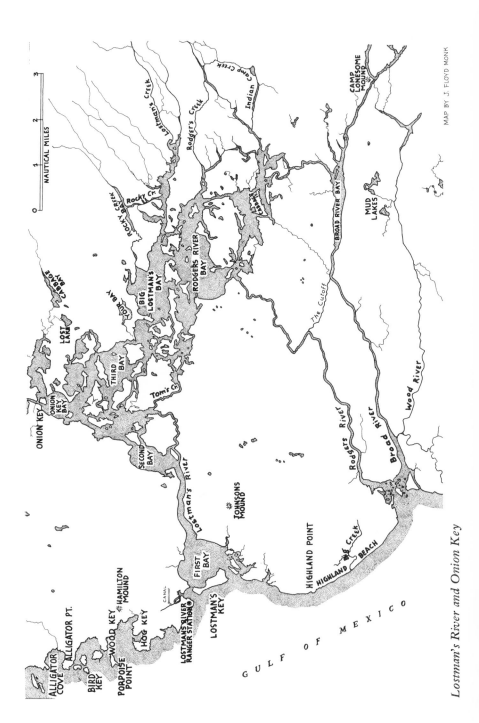

Lostman's River and Onion Key

MAP BY J. FLOYD MONK

shore. He found three sailors (not five soldiers) who had jumped ship at Key West and had hired a man to take them to the mainland. When the boatman saw smoke on the horizon toward Key West and suspected pursuit by the Navy, he had put them ashore three days before. Allen had entered their names in his log as John, Bill, and Sam Lostman—hence Lostman's Key and Lostman's River.

A yachtsman on a west coast cruise related that on March 4, 1886 his party had rowed up "Lost-Man's" River two miles or more to "the solitary plantation of one man living on that stream." The following year another party including A. E. Douglass followed a row of stakes across the bay and found Joseph B. Camp living at what must have been the same location. Camp told Douglass that they were the first visitors he had ever had.

Douglass also reported considerable activity in the region, noting that a number of Key West merchants had hired people to occupy and cultivate land there to produce vegetables for the market. A reconnaissance party for the Coast and Geodetic Survey in 1891 reported what seemed to be abandoned fields along Rodgers River, and one small schooner whose owner was cutting buttonwood. The Dimocks referred to these fields as abandoned sugar plantations in the early 1900's. The term "plantation" was used by residents on that coast to designate farming operations of any size. All farming was on shell mounds as there was no dry land in the area as there was at Everglades, Cape Sable, and Flamingo.

There was much movement of settlers in the area, and this was accomplished more easily than one might suppose. People usually had only squatters' rights to property and that was often not established legally. They frequently sold their land to newcomers, or just abandoned it in the search for new areas for woodcutting, fishing, hunting, or to search for a new bit of suitable farm land. Moving consisted of loading the meager family possessions on a boat, sailing to a new site, and there erecting another palmetto thatch shack; all this could be done in a relatively short time. The problem of obtaining fresh water was solved partly by catching rain water that ran off the "roof," as was done in more substantial homes as well. Often families had a permanent home in a larger settlement like Chokoloskee Island and made temporary camps in the islands while they were fishing, hunting, farming, or cutting wood.

Clam diggers established temporary bases on nearby keys while they gathered clams for the canneries at Caxambas and Marco. The shallow water areas, up to about waist-deep, were reserved for individual workers, and the deeper water was worked by dredges. The diggers encased their feet in canvas moccasins that protected them from sharp objects but permitted them at the same time to feel the clams underfoot. When one was located, the digger would reach down with a clam fork, lift it up, and drop it into a skiff riding alongside.

The 1910 hurricane caught twenty-two men on Plover Key, which stands seven or eight feet above normal high tide. The storm took all but three of their boats. After the storm they made their way back, with some difficulty, to Caxambas, which was also wrecked by wind and water.

Little Pavilion Key, not identified on maps, is a very small sandy island north of Pavilion Key that was much frequented by clam diggers. As many as seventy-five people stayed there at times, living in tiny shacks built on stilts. They usually left these areas in the face of storm threat. In 1926 twenty-five men appeared at Chatham Bend during the hurricane. They had left Pavilion Key in a clam boat that had broken up in the storm. Three days later one man who had refused to attempt to escape to the mainland was rescued.

Another early settler was James Houston Hamilton Hopkins, who came from north Georgia. He had fought in the Confederate army at the age of sixteen, after which he married and became the father of three children. Things did not go well for him and he went to Texas for a time to escape his bad luck and responsibilities. He then came to Florida, going first to Cedar Key where he dropped the name of Hopkins and shed the liabilities associated with it. As James Hamilton, he then moved to Fort Myers where he married "Gene Ballard's sister," name unknown, and moved on down the coast to the Lostman's River area. From this marriage three sons, Frank, Lewis, and Jesse, were born, and one daughter, Gertrude, who later married John Henry Thompson. Like so many others they were farmers, fishermen, and hunters each in season. They did not remain very long at Lostman's River but they and their children remained on the west coast of the lower peninsula.

Any accessible hammock was prized for its agricultural possibilities, as hammock land was high enough to be relatively free from flooding by salt water and, more importantly, it was usually very fertile. About 1904 or 1905 the elder Hamilton with his son Jesse and his son-in-law cleared a road to Johnson's Hammock. This site was an old shell mound which was also known locally as Royal Palm Hammock from the fine stand of royal palms growing there. It also had been known as Smith Hammock after a hunter who once established a camp there; its final name was derived from another resident, Johnnie Johnson, a trapper and hunter who lived there for two years.

Hamilton and his party pushed up to the head of a small creek, went ashore, and cut a right of way southeastward through the mangrove swamp to the hammock. They started to dig a ditch alongside the road, using the soil to build up the roadbed into which they had already thrown the brush they had cut to clear the path. Though they never completed the ditch, others extended it farther out along the road. Hamilton moved a horse and wagon over the road and removed from the mound on the hammock enough shell to make what Thompson remembered as a "fair shell road." All this was done to produce a crop of tomatoes and get them out to market. Little evidence of the road now remains, but there is a distinctly outlined right of way leading to the hammock. Apparently seventy five or more royal palms were brought out from the hammock by this same route.

In the early 1890's Henry Smith from Wauchula and two half-brothers, Leland and Frank Rice, came to the lower Gulf coast. The Rice brothers achieved notoriety in 1915 when, in company with two others, they robbed the Homestead Bank and fled to the swamps east of Chokoloskee. Leland was shot and killed resisting arrest. Frank was shot but recovered to serve a long jail term. Henry Smith married Virginia Myers, whose father Philip had been a Civil War prisoner at Fort Jefferson. When released he returned to Georgia, married there, and later came to Tampa and, later still, to Russell Island three miles south of Everglades in upper Turner's River. There Mrs. Myers died and is buried with "eight or ten" others on the island. Philip moved to Key West and remarried there, but his four children remained in the Ten Thousand Islands. A descendant explains that they left Russell Island, but like many of their contemporaries lived at one time or another on most of the habitable islands in the area. The four daughters married Daniels, Gardner, Gandees, and Smith men—all prominently associated with early life at Half Way Creek and Fakahatchee Island, and only less so at numerous other sites.

Far more intimately associated with the Lostman's River area is the family of Richard Hamilton, who came into the region somewhat earlier but did not move down the coast until about 1900. Richard Hamilton had served in the Civil War, fighting among other places in the Battle of Natural Bridge to defend Tallahassee at the very end of the war. By the family's account he was mustered out at Punta Gorda, went to sea from Key West for five years, and then remained in Key West another two years. He then moved to Pine Level, near Arcadia, Florida, where he first married. To this union four sons and a daughter were born, but they play little part in our story.

Richard Hamilton then moved to Everglades and became associated with William Smith Allen, founder of the town of Everglades on Allen (now Barron) River. There Hamilton married a daughter of John Weeks, to whom three sons and three daughters were born. The family, like many others, moved about frequently. While they lived at Chatham Bend, the place Ed Watson later made famous, Eugene, Walter, and Mary were born. Leon was born during a brief residence at Fakahatchee Island. They lived for a time on Possum Key before Jean Chevelier gave it his name. In 1895 they lived on Mormon Key at the mouth of Chatham River, and two daughters, Annie and Agnes, were born there. Some say Mormon Key got its name from Hamilton, who lived there with one of his two living wives. In the late nineties Hamilton traded his Mormon Key claim to Ed Watson and moved to Flamingo for a two year stay to be near his wife's father.

When Nicholas Santini left his long established homestead on Chokoloskee Island near the end of the century and moved to Miami, Richard Hamilton acquired his claim on Hog Key just above the mouth of Lostman's River. Thereafter Hamilton and his sons were closely identified with that general area. Hog Key was named for the hogs raised there, which Hamilton descendants recall had meat that was inedible, tasting of the oysters and crabs the hogs ate. Pigs kept in pens and fed table scraps and garden and field food, however, made fine pork.

In 1901, Hamilton's three sons, Walter, Eugene, and Leon, moved to Wood Key (sometimes referred to as Porpoise Point— a feature of the key) to establish a fishing ranch. The term "ranch" is a survival from the Spanish *ranchos* that were established all along the Gulf coast to catch, salt, and dry fish for the Havana market. The term "ranchos" is still in common parlance in the area today. Twice a week the brothers sent to Key West eight to ten barrels of dried fish, which was shipped from there to Cuba. Using a two-inch mesh net 150 yards long, they could easily catch more fat mullet than they could handle. In about 1905 fish houses began to be built; these were serviced by runboats which brought in ice and took away the catch. These soon put an end to the salting and drying operations of the Hamilton brothers, but they remained commercial fishermen.

The location of a fish house at the mouth of Lostman's River made it a gathering place for commercial fishermen, many of whom lived there at least temporarily in palmetto shacks on shore or on board their boats. The Hamiltons had permanent homes there. They each played some musical instrument and old Leon laughingly recalls that when they met for a Saturday night frolic they really had themselves a "ball"—if not a brawl.

The 1910 hurricane, the worst on that coast until Donna came along fifty years later, found four families living on Wood Key. Eugene Hamilton was on the northeast end; next was Gilbert Johnson, a Nassau "Conch" who had married a Georgia girl he met in Key West. The third was Richard Hamilton and the fourth was Leon Hamilton, who had married Sarah, the daughter of the Johnsons. They rode out the storm in boats on the lee of the island while the water broke across it. The whole south side of the island was swept clean, and only Eugene Hamilton rebuilt his home there. The other three moved into the Lostman's River area to re-establish their homes.

Van Campen Heilner visited the region with Eugene Hamil-

ton as his guide, and in *Field and Stream*, January, 1919, told
of his encounters with great numbers of alligators and fish, the
principal object of his trip. He also visited a hermit named
Jorkans who lived several miles back of Gene's place and
bought some potatoes from him. Jorkans had traveled as far
away as China and Japan before settling there. Heilner won-
dered why he chose that life but, true to the code of the
region, made no possibly embarrassing inquiries.

Today the southern side of Wood Key has all the appearance
of an old field, with many palms and other plants remaining to
mark homesites abandoned half a century ago. The only schoolhouse ever known to exist there was once on Wood Key.
Eugene Hamilton remembers that a visiting yachtsman named
Littleton provided the building, a prefabricated barn ordered
from Sears and Roebuck. Monroe County provided the school's
teacher, but the school was discontinued after the 1910 hurricane. Such schooling as the children got thereafter was received
at Chokoloskee or Everglades, where youngsters were sometimes sent for short stays. Leon Hamilton recalls, however, that
at one time "Old Man Ellis," who was hiding out, stayed with
his family for a while and taught his children.

Leon's home on the river was situated on a little sandy beach
a few hundred yards long, on the east bank near the mouth of

Leon Hamilton's Place, Lostman's River

Walter Hamilton's Place, Lostman's River

the river where storms alternately eroded and built up the small area of low beach. Eugene's house was on the west bank at the mouth of the river on a shell mound where there was some evidence of Indian occupation. The site today, after being rearranged by Hurricane Donna, may bear little resemblance to the original land. The storm moved much of the shell that made up the river front to the back of the area, doing some damage to the small ranger station established there by the Park Service. The storm turned up very few artifacts on this mound, in contrast to the numbers found elsewhere, raising some question as to whether it ever was an important Indian site. Back of this area was a ten acre "plantation" to which some promoters cut a canal in the 1920's. A rusting iron pot set in a furnace built of worm rock (which is found only along that coast) marks the spot where the Hamiltons grew sugar cane on a large mound in Farm Creek. Walter Hamilton's place about four miles up river on the left bank is now marked by a banana tree on a "bluff" some two feet higher than the surrounding swamp.

James Henry Thompson lived on Lostman's River at Highland Beach in 1910. He and his wife and one small child lived in a typical palmetto shack and he fished in nearby waters. His experience there illustrates the fact that boats were often the safest refuge in storms. When the wind began to reach dangerous velocity and rising waters threatened to overflow his homesite, he placed his wife and a few possessions in the skiff he used for fishing, put a tin tub over the baby on the net board, pushed the skiff out into the mangrove swamp, and rode out the storm there. In September, 1960, many people in Everglades rode out the hurricane in boats that they anchored in protected channels in the nearby mangrove forest.

When the Park was created in 1947, Walter Hamilton had been dead for ten years and except for Eugene and Leon, who still lived there, the rest of the family had abandoned the river. Eugene and Leon moved from within Park boundaries. Ten years later old Leon, then 75 years of age, still felt that he did not want to revisit the old homestead unless he could stay. He later became reconciled to his new life and enjoyed visits to the scenes of his earlier life. His, like others, seems to us a hard life. He had rebuilt his home after the 1910 and 1926 hurricanes and after a tornado in 1940. He had farmed a bit, hunted in season, and guided fishing and hunting parties occasionally when visiting yachts had found safe anchorage in his part of the river. He had primarily been a commercial fisherman and could think of no better life.

He recalled that once around 1920 when the family needed some dental work they spent about three days building a palmetto shack and then brought the dentist down from Chokoloskee for a visit. Those who had ordered dentures met the dentist a few weeks later in town. They had no church or store, but in the early days occasionally had the services of a passing priest. The three Hamiltons reared their families on the river, and some of the younger generation stayed for a time. One of Leon's daughters, Mary, married Johnnie Gray. The couple started out with a palmetto shack but soon brought lumber and metal roofing from the abandoned bark factory at Shark River and built a more substantial house. A few years later they moved to Mormon Key. Eventually they moved to Chokoloskee where they carried the mail to and from the post office at Everglades by boat. When the road to the mainland was opened in 1955 they carried the mail by car. Later they moved to Jerome, where Gray died.

Like most of the other settlers, the Hamiltons had only squatters' rights at first, using the land as they used the nearby waters. The completely unrestrained use of the land and its resources so conditioned the attitudes of those who lived in the Park area that it was difficult for them to accept the new regulations and laws that restricted that use. As one man who grew up in the region put it, "What's wrong with killing white ibis? I was raised on fish and white ibis." Presumably the three Hamilton brothers were the only residents there in 1925 when D. A. McDougal acquired the land by purchase from the Palgrove Company that had owned it for two decades. The three brothers were each given a deed to ten acres around his homesite by the new owner. By 1947 only Leon still owned his; the other two had reverted to the state for taxes.

Three miles below the mouth of the river is another picturesque little sand beach with a bit of higher land behind it. This is called Lostman's Beach locally but appears as Highland Beach on the map. It is best known as the home of the Rewis family who lived twenty-seven years in the area, much of the time on this beach. Back of Highland Beach is a shell mound about five miles long that has much the appearance of an old ocean beach; a road leads to it from the north end of the beach. It too was cultivated and the native royal palms were removed. The beach is now marked by a stand of Australian pines not native to the Park. Rewis planted coconut trees there but they fell to the 1926 hurricane. He later replaced his house but not the trees, and who planted the pines is not known. Rewis also had a place of about two acres, known as the Ellis field, up Harney River.

Three of the long succession of families that from time to time lived on Rodgers River can be identified as living there around 1900. About one and a half miles up the river on the west bank was Livingston Atwell, son of Shelton Atwell, who lived half a mile farther up on the same side. The third, another mile and a half farther, is recalled simply as Mr. Evans.

Others known to have lived on Rodgers River at one time or another were John Demery, Charles Cross, and a Dr. Harris whose home was in Key West. Charles Torrey Simpson reported a trip to the abandoned Evans place in 1923; he mentioned twenty five royal palms all recently destroyed, presumably by a storm, and two beautiful "plantations."

Edward Atwell, another of Shelton's ten children, now lives in Miami. He recalls that farming was done on a series of parallel ridges back from the river, producing sugarcane which was sold in Key West. Once when the high water of a storm killed their cane the father and son went to Ed Watson for seed cane to replant the fields. Watson entertained them royally for four days—another instance of neighbors who remember the "bad man" of that country in only the kindliest way. The Atwells also grew pumpkins, Irish and sweet potatoes, onions, watermelons, and huge cabbages. (So rich was the soil that nobody on that coast ever grew any ordinary-sized cabbages!) There was also a little house on stilts in a creek at Tarpon Bay where, Edward recalls, "The rich land would grow anything." The water was fresh almost to the mouth of the river except in driest times, and alligators and deer were plentiful. The twenty-five year stay of the Atwells on Rodgers River ended suddenly about 1901 when Edward's mother announced that she had had enough and that she was going to Key West, never to return. The family yielded to her ultimatum.

Broad River is rarely mentioned as a place of settlement. Oddly enough, though, it is reported that Joe Wiggins had a store—possibly a floating one—there early in this century. He had kept store at Wiggins Pass, to which he gave his name. In 1883 he moved to Allen River, and three years later to Sandfly Pass, where he traded with Indians and passing neighbors. The Santini diaries contain numerous mentions of visits to Joe Wiggins. Keeping a store, of course, merely meant keeping in his home a supply of the staple items he and his neighbors used.

Lostman's River was the scene of one of Florida's most spectacular real estate promotions in the middle twenties. The Tropical Development Company, a Miami concern, acquired three sections (3, 4, 9 and part of 16, Township 56 South,

Range 31, East) of land astride the mouth of Lostman's River, and laid out on paper—but did not survey—Poinciana, as a future subdivision. Poinciana appears on the Monroe County tax rolls as "Poinciana Mainland" to distinguish it from a smaller but active subdivision on one of the Florida Keys. On Lostman's River, 6,756 lots were returned to state ownership for delinquent taxes, but the 1960 tax roll showed 2,177 as still privately owned. This does not mean that the present owners have held the lots since the mid-twenties, for delinquent tax sales cause many changes in ownership. Park officials wonder how to go about contacting the many private owners in order to acquire the lots for Park property.

Onion Key, only an acre in extent and lying about ten miles from the mouth of Lostman's River, became the field headquarters for the Poinciana development in 1925. As the story goes the key got its name when an unidentified man who wished to escape even the limited exposure he faced on the Gulf front moved to the key with his wife, built a shack, cleared a portion of the land, and grew onions there. Recent excavations by John W. Griffin, archaeologist for the southeastern region of the National Park Service, reveal that the island has a long history of Indian occupation, probably of at least a thousand years duration and apparently covering most of the island's surface.

Onion Key lies opposite the mouth of Plate Creek, the only inland waterway from the river northward up the Gulf coast, and was certainly an important way station. When William R. Catlow, Erben Cook, and others were surveying land lines in the region in the early 1920's, they recalled that it was not a mangrove-type key; the shoreline rose straight from the water and was overgrown with large buttonwood trees. The settler who cleared the land for farming reportedly found a quantity of brass buttons and some coins in a hole in a tree trunk about five feet above ground when he was cutting up a log—indicating again how little we know of much of the early history of the Park region.

The company did a little dredging on the shore, built some docks, and brought in a number of portable buildings. There was a radio shack to house communication equipment and an electric light plant. They relied chiefly on advertising to sell the lots, but also brought in prospective buyers by boat from Miami and nearby stations on the Florida East Coast Railroad. The Tamiami Trail at that time had been constructed west from Miami to the Dade County line, and the Chevelier Corporation was building the "Loop Road" west into northern Monroe County. Visitors to Poinciana drove to a point about two miles west of Pinecrest, from which they then walked six miles south to a canoe landing on a branch of the upper part of Lostman's River known as Lostman's 5. There they boarded a boat of some sort and made their way to Onion Key, a distance of about a mile, to reach the area billed as "The Coming Miami of the Gulf." Some of the advertising was highly imaginative and some of the statements were without foundation in fact. A map showed a road projected from the Old Chevelier Road at Forty Mile Bend southwestwardly to the site, but no promise was included as to when it would be built, nor was it mentioned that if it were constructed it would have to consist mainly of causeways or bridges.

In the *Illustrated Daily Tab*, a Miami boom-time newspaper, the following statements appeared in an advertisement on January 5, 1926 for the Poinciana lots:

> History tells us that the first bananas were brought to Poinciana over a hundred years ago when the original Spanish settlement was formed here. Today the groves the Spaniards planted, the bananas, oranges, limes, and coconuts are still flourishing and producing fruit of excellent size and flavor—proof of the wonderful fertility of the soil.

The land boom collapsed and was buried with the 1926 hurricane. Captain Thomas Annadown, who owned and operated the trading schooner *Ina* in the region between 1917 and 1935, worked for the Poinciana Company for a time. He was wise in the ways of storms and took aboard all of his possessions, advised others to do likewise, and sailed up a creek to ride out the hurricane. He returned after the storm had passed and left for the record a remarkable pair of "before and after" photo-

Poinciana Company headquarters on Onion Key before and after the 1926 hurricane

Shark River Country

graphs that tell a graphic story of the destruction wrought. Leon Hamilton recalled taking the "Poinciana crowd" back to Miami and of their hopeful—perhaps defiant—declarations that they were not quitting; they would be back. Captain Annadown (known as "Anchordown" to some of his jesting friends) transported some of the workers to Miami, paid them their wages, and brought back lumber and tarpaper for rebuilding. A remnant of the employees moved the power plant to the Eugene Hamilton place, where the ranger station now stands, and constructed a few tarpaper shacks. The company hopefully advertised that all was not lost and that the promised improvements would be completed. But whatever chance Poinciana ever had for development had gone with the wind. Purchasers there and elsewhere in Florida lost their enthusiasm. It is difficult to look at the small island in the river today and realize that it was once the heart of an enterprise that sold thousands of nearby lots to people all over the country.

Shark River, the southernmost of the Gulf coast rivers which drain the Everglades, is the deepest and longest but affords the least land above sea level. In a sense it is not a part of the complex of interwoven rivers and bays on that coast for it is connected to none of them. It, along with the Little Shark and the Harney, provide access to Whitewater Bay and the region north of the Cape Sable prairie. It has always been possible, sometimes with the aid of a short portage in times of low water, to cross the lower peninsula to the east coast by this route. Another stream in this area that is both long and deep but provides no outlet from Whitewater Bay is Joe River, which runs from the east end of the bay along the south shore and breaks up in the islands as it approaches Shark River.

Only two or three bits of land along the Shark River have ever been mentioned as being inhabited. The principal one, also used by Indians as a camping site, is at Little Banana Patch at the head of the river. Banana trees grow there and several attempts at farming have been reported. Kirk Munroe told of charcoal burners on one island that must have been visited by many other people in the early 1800's. Andrew Canova mentioned having camped on an island about eight miles upriver in the late 1850's in the Seminole War, and having walked around in the nearby forest. Canova may have been on another river unless these islands have "come and gone," as it is scarcely possible now to find any area above water except at Banana Patch or Avocado Mound, where there is no nearby "forest." Others who used the river extensively had their bases on Little Sable Creek at Northwest Cape, where there was dry land and fresh water.

The Manetta Company early in this century engaged in a major effort to extract tannic acid from the great mangrove forest, principally along the Shark, and also thought that the tall straight trees as much as sixteen inches in diameter might produce hardwood lumber of excellent quality and beauty.

Only the raw material was present. Machinery, labor, supplies, and even drinking water had to be brought in by boat; the drinking water came from farther up the river where it was always fresh in those early days. The nearest bases of supplies were at Miami, Key West, or Tampa, with lesser sources at Chokoloskee, Everglades, or Fort Myers. The first step was the building of a two and one half acre platform on pilings to raise the operation above the mangrove swamp in which it was located about a mile upriver. The work began in 1904 and three years later offices and quarters for white employees, machine sheds, maintenance shops, and drying sheds for the bark were ready. Upriver a series of houses on stilts provided homes for the Negro labor brought in to cut the trees and strip off the bark. Others, principally residents of the coastal area who served as boat operators, pilots, and guides, often lived on their own boats or lighters.

The Manetta Company had first been established in 1904 on the Miami River; from there the mangrove trees in the most accessible areas such as Miami Beach had been stripped of bark. In early 1908 three barge loads of machinery were moved to the newly prepared site at Shark River and the vastly greater supply of raw material. The tannic acid content was high but the cost of production proved also to be high. The effort to use the trees for lumber failed. No means could be found to dry the boards without their cracking and that aspect of the project was dropped. The 1910 hurricane brought all operations to

Mangrove bark factory, Shark River

an abrupt halt and no immediate effort thereafter was made to reconstruct the factory. A passerby in 1911 described the area as "a bold, strong etching of the ruins of despair. . . . It was simply a junk dealer's back yard." Two white men and two Negroes then constituted the entire population.

The Manetta Company later resumed production and continued it intermittently until 1923. Edward Atwell, who spent his boyhood on Rodgers River, recalls working for the company from 1916 to the closing of the operations. Van Campen Heilner reported a visit to the factory, probably in 1919, when he played a Victor phonograph "for the poor fellows who were there," one of whom had never heard such a music-making machine. As few as four men worked there at times during World War I. Heilner reported that fresh water was scarce when he was there in March. Atwell recalls that they could usually get fresh water in or above Tarpon Bay, but already the effects of Everglades drainage were being felt in the lowered volume of water flowing that way. The company substituted a diesel engine for its two steam boilers because of the difficulty of providing enough fresh water for them.

Atwell vividly recalls the mosquitoes and how the men painted the wire of their screens with oil to keep out the sand flies. The men lived on boats until the two-story living quarters on shore were provided. When they got up mornings they crawled from the mosquito bars and ran up and down the beach while they dressed to avoid the swarms of mosquitoes. Though Atwell when interviewed in 1966 in Miami was a hardy seventy eight and able to work every day, he believed that years of breathing smoke from the black mangrove smudge pot permanently damaged his lungs.

During the hearings in the 1940's to condemn land for Park purposes, the company's owners testified that they had ceased operations there only because other sources of raw material were more accessible, implying that one day they might find it feasible to return to Shark River where the bark was of such high acid content and in such great quantity. Barron Collier bought some of the Manetta Company machinery for use in his development at Everglades. Residents along the coast salvaged much of the timber and sheet metal to build houses for themselves. The remainder gradually rotted away until today few signs remain on the riverfront. The remnants of an old barge lie in a nearby creek and Hurricane Donna uncovered the two abandoned steam boilers resting in mud back in the mangrove.

Remains of bark factory, 1960

H. P. Rutherford, a Homestead lumberman, experimented for years with mangrove wood, seeking some commercial use for it. It was heavy, hard, and took on a high polish, and he felt it would be ideal for shuttles for textile looms. But it lacked the appeal if not the qualities of the more accessible dogwood and persimmon, and the use of natural woods was also beginning to be threatened by developments in plastics. In 1953 the Florida Internal Improvement Board, which has the management of the state's public lands, leased 16,600 acres of the upper mangrove coast to the Mangrove Products Corporation, a Rutherford Company, for thirty years. This lease caused much dissension by those who anticipated that this land was one day to be acquired for the Park. That controversy, and the possibility of a very long waiting period before mangrove could be profitably marketed, apparently induced Rutherford and his associates to allow the lease to lapse. He and others have continued to experiment with mangrove as a source of fertilizer and as food for animals. Since deer thrived on it, it was theorized that cattle might also be fed with meal made from mangrove leaves. If uses are found for sawgrass and mangrove there could indeed be a mighty harvest in the entire Everglades and southern coastal areas.

The mangrove forest remains practically intact, partially killed at times by hurricanes but usually growing back to assert its control of the coastal area—and possibly even to enlarge it eventually. When "Old Man Darwin" finally gives up his homestead on Possum Key only a patch of exotic plants in the wilderness here and there on a key, hammock, or riverbank will mark the more than half century of white man's life in the Ten Thousand Islands and on the mangrove coast in the Park.

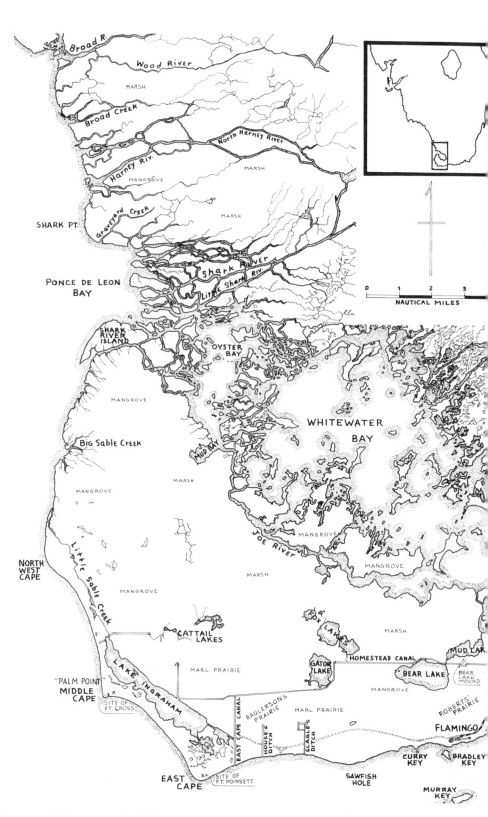

VI

Down At the Cape

MAN'S LIFE ON THE CAPE was different from that in the Ten Thousand Islands and on the mangrove coast only as the physical features differed and altered the natural setting. There were no rivers here to give access to the interior, and no protecting fringe of islands such as the west coast provided. Water ran deep near the shore but the unbroken coastline offered little safe anchorage from storms. The only access by water to Lake Ingraham before the early 1920's was by the long, shallow, narrow, crooked, and overgrown Little Sable Creek, but Big and Little Sable Creeks did provide some refuge in heavy weather.

The distinguishing feature of the Cape area is the long curving sand beach that borders the coastline in serried ridges and extends inland less than a hundred yards. Lake Ingraham, which looks as if it might once have been part of the ocean before being cut off by a sand ridge thrown up by a storm, lies behind Middle Cape and East Cape. North of Lake Ingraham and extending eastward to Flamingo is the Cape Sable prairie, a broad strip of marl that is marshy in rainy seasons. The western part of the prairie is commonly known as Raulerson Prairie and the eastern end as Roberts or Flamingo Prairie. Between the prairie and the Shark River—Whitewater Bay water complex is a wide band of wet, marshy, mangrove-covered land. In dry times, before it was intersected by canals, it was possible to drive across this land almost to the Shark River basin. The 1928 Coast and Geodetic Survey map shows a trail running westward from Flamingo across the prairie, skirting Lake Ingraham on the north shore and ending on Little Sable Creek. In the 1930's a road following essentially the same route was built by Department of Agriculture work crews. This road, which bridged the canals that had been cut across the old trail, was usable in dry seasons until 1954.

The soil of the prairie looks and is fertile but the sandy beach in front is relatively sterile. The first white men to record their impressions of the prairie concluded that it would be an excellent site for farming and ranching; they also assumed that it must have been cultivated by Indians in earlier times. Bernard Romans reported, "at Sandy Point, the southern extremity of the peninsula, are old fields being the land formerly planted by the Calusa savages. . . ." He called an area about fifteen miles north "Upper Comanche fields." This assumption, among other things, gave rise to the notion, now refuted by anthropologists, that the Calusa Indians practiced agriculture.

Attractive as the land appears there is little evidence, archaeological or historical, to indicate that the prairie was ever occupied permanently by either Indians or white men until after the middle of the nineteenth century. There are a few small Indian mounds in the mangrove swamp to the north, but they do not indicate long residence or extensive use. The same may be said of similar remains on the keys in Florida Bay. Perhaps the frequency of storm waves washing over the land not only discouraged occupation but scattered the evidence of what little there may have been. Also, since living was peculiarly easy in the region, the mere presence of arable soil did not necessitate its utilization for agriculture.

White men from the days of discovery certainly fished in the nearby waters and possibly dried fish on the Cape's sandy beaches. Hunters came from the lower Florida Keys for the abundance of game long before Florida became part of the United States. Mariners came ashore to get fresh water as they did at similar beaches in Central and South America and the West Indies.

Potable water was found in shallow wells on Cape Sable's sand beaches. Loren Roberts of Flamingo described these wells as cased with two barrels, indicating a depth of not more than six or seven feet. He commented, "You can't pump 'em dry, but if you go too deep you'll hit salt." Two explanations for this are possible. One is that water was trapped in shallow depressions covered over with marl on the bottom before being filled with sand by a storm. The other is that rain water held in the sand floated on top of the salt water beneath.

A number of these beach wells were widely known as reliable sources of water. Caxambas on Marco Island got its name from *cacimba* (place of wells), a word used all over Spanish America to denote such spots. Other well known wells were at Cape Romano, Gomez Key, Lostman's Key, Little Sable Creek, Bahia Honda, and Lower Matecumbe. When John James Audubon visited Florida Bay in 1831 and 1832 he reported at the end of a visit to Sandy Key, "Having filled our casks from a well long since dug in the sand of Cape Sable either by Seminole Indians or Pirates, no matter which, we left the sand isle."

Richard Moore, with his father, a brother, and a sister lived briefly on their boat on Little Sable Creek in the early nineties, having found a safe anchorage and fresh water there. The well was frequented by spongers, fishermen, and wood cutters in the area. Herbert K. Job, writing of his experience at Flamingo in 1903 commented, "A dry and thirsty land is Cape Sable, with all its swamps, overflowed as they are by the sea, and no drinking water to be had, save from the clouds. Our water barrels were nearly empty so one night, when a vessel had been secured, we dropped off the soap flat and south westward around Cape Sable and up near 'Middle Cape' where we found a tolerable well from which to fill our casks."

Along the Gulf coast it was often possible simply to go up the rivers to find fresh water—except in dry seasons on the shorter rivers. Chokoloskee Island residents went up the Turner River or over to Cape Romano for water, and the tanbark factory on Shark River was supplied by sending boats upriver past the salt line.

Residents on occasion and in emergencies also distilled fresh water from the salt or brackish water available. After the 1910 hurricane either destroyed or salted their cisterns at Flamingo, Mrs. Loren Roberts and Louis Loudon recall that they and others made stills of fifty gallon oil barrels and, using buttonwood for fuel, operated them for several months until their cisterns could be rebuilt and another rainy season filled them. Hunting parties in the Whitewater Bay region sometimes carried along small stills as part of the regular equipment stowed in the glades skiffs in which they traveled. They used fifty-pound lard cans or similar metal containers for distilling purposes, and stored supplies in the cans when not in use. These cans, which had tight fitting lids, were much in demand as they provided the driest storage facility available.

The Seminole Wars did much to call attention to the Cape Sable region. Six months after the conflict started in North Florida some alarmed inhabitants of Key West wrote to Commodore Alexander J. Dallas and warned him that Indians were collecting in the Cape Sable area only "twenty miles away." It was said their fires could be seen from the island and that parties of straggling Indians were frequently seen between the Keys and the mainland.

Military and civil authorities were still convinced that Seminoles were in frequent contact with Spanish fishermen on the west coast and at Cape Sable and were buying arms and ammunition. Some believed that the Indians were supplied with weapons to enlist the aid of the Indians against any interference with their fishing along the coast by United States military authorities.

On December 30, 1838, Surgeon General Thomas Lawson, commanding Florida Volunteers on a reconnaissance of the lower west coast, proposed that the whole lower peninsula be occupied by settlers to hold the Indians in check. He pointed out as good sites for settlements areas near Marco Sound, Cape Romano, and Pavilion (now Chatham) River, and the banks of Shark River and "Lake Manatee [possibly Tarpon Bay] ten miles still further east." He saw in Cape Sable an ideal spot for a military post and depot for a colony that should be established on the prairie and nearby islands. They might, he wrote, produce grain, vegetables, sugar, cotton, and rice, "etc." and they would certainly cut out the intercourse between the Indians and the Spanish fishermen and possibly others from the British West Indies islands.

Fort Poinsett was established by Lawson on East Cape in 1838 and Fort Cross by an unnamed officer at Middle Cape during the Third Seminole War—probably in 1856. There is no record of any remains of the fort at Middle Cape. Since the forts were constructed mostly of logs and sand, the wood eventually disintegrated and the sand was scattered, but until the 1935 hurricane swept across East Cape, outlines of the Fort Poinsett ditches remained to mark the spot. Mrs. Carrie Douthit, who went to the Cape as a child of seven early in this century, recalled playing in the ditches and around the heaps of sand that had been associated with the fort. The last metal objects such as round shot and scattered unrelated items have disappeared only in recent years.

Reports of the presence of Indians were undoubtedly exaggerated, and there is no sound evidence of contact by them with Spanish or British traders in arms. Chief Chekika and the "Spanish Indians" who raided Indian Key, however, were certainly in the vicinity.

At about the end of the Seminole Wars and prior to the Mexican War, an ambitious program of coastal defenses aimed primarily to protect commerce was initiated by the United States government. Fort Taylor at Key West and Fort Jefferson on Garden Key in the Dry Tortugas were parts of a chain of military installations that reached from Maine to Texas. Settlers viewed these forts as giving them better security from Indian attacks, and slaveholders may also have been assisted by the military. The boat of Johnathan Walker, a Massachusetts abolitionist, carrying seven runaway slaves from Pensacola to the Bahamas was stopped off Key West. Walker became something of a national figure when Florida courts sentenced him to stand in the pillory, to be branded on the hand with the letters "S.S." and to pay a fine of $300 and serve a term of imprisonment for each slave he had assisted to flee. His friends paid his fines and had him released from prison. John Greenleaf Whittier wrote a poem, "The Branded Hand," about the situation, and Walker wrote a book by the same title recounting his experiences.

Before they were completed the forts proved to be obsolete, but federal troops occupied Fort Taylor in the Civil War and ammunition was stored there in the Spanish-American War. Fort Jefferson became a federal military prison and was made famous by the presence of Dr. Samuel Alexander Mudd, who had treated the injured leg of John Wilkes Booth following the assassination of President Lincoln. It was for a time also used as a quarantine station.

During the Spanish-American War, when storage facilities at Key West proved inadequate and channels were too shallow for large ships to approach closer than six miles, the coal sheds at Fort Jefferson were reconditioned and some new ones built and used until facilities could be developed at Key West. Fort Jefferson was garrisoned briefly in World War I, after which, for all practical purposes, it was abandoned until 1935 when President Franklin D. Roosevelt declared it a national monument.

Many officials, particularly military men, believed the habitable mainland should be settled by loyal white men who could supply manpower and supplies for forts in the area; they considered the South Florida coast extremely exposed and vulnerable.

Colonel William S. Harney of Seminole War fame was among those who urged that the Everglades be drained and settled, and he himself at one time seriously considered settling at Cape Sable. A letter written in February, 1857 while he was on an official visit to Fort Poinsett, which was reactivated for the final

Fort Jefferson, Dry Tortugas

phase of the Seminole War, was addressed to Florida's Senator David Yulee and read in part.:

My dear Sir:

I visited Cape Sable a few days since there is a Depot for the troops operating in the Everglades & c.–and have fallen quite in love with it–so much so that I am determined to purchase it if I possibly can, & at once commence a Fruit and Sugar Plantation. Can you do me the favor to get an order to have it surveyed at once, so that I can employ men to commence in clearing and Planting at once? There are three points & I would say these are about fifteen hundred or two thousand acres in all, just enough for a small plantation such as I want.

What reply he received is not known, but he did not establish the Cape Sable plantation and the survey was not made until another half century had passed. Possibly the outbreak of the Civil War diverted Harney's attention.

Henry Bateman Goodyear, brother of Charles A. Goodyear who invented the process of vulcanizing rubber, is said to have once scouted Cape Sable and made great plans for a rubber plantation there, probably based on the idea that the sap of some native plant might be used or that some rubber-producing plant could be introduced. Later when Henry Ford and Harvey Firestone visited Charles A. Edison at Fort Myers, speculation arose as to whether the trio might be working on a scheme to make rubber from some plant in the lower peninsula.

There is little reference to the Cape in official records of the American Civil War. We may assume that ships of the Gulf Blockading Squadron based at Key West found little occasion to visit isolated areas when they patrolled the coast. Small Confederate crafts no doubt took refuge in the maze of channels on the mangrove coast but they were too far removed from the sources of supply and markets to play important roles in blockade running.

In a "History of the Ten Thousand Islands" published serially in the *Fort Myers Press* and other local papers in 1927, C. Roy Watson stated that Union army officials from Key West had farmers working at Cape Sable. The city was overrun with refugees and food was scarce. The government reportedly provided seed and tools and the farmers did well for a time. This may have been the first instance of farming on the mainland for the Key West market. Certainly there was more or less continuous occupation and cultivation of at least a limited sort after that time. The greatest setbacks must have occurred when occasional storms swept sea water over the low-lying land and salted it; the farming would then have to be suspended until rains could leach out the salt. This desalting, however, often occurred in the final phases of a storm when heavy rainfall may occur after the storm tides subside.

At the close of the war when President Jefferson Davis of the Confederacy and some members of his cabinet fled southward, watchful federal officials suspected they might escape to Havana by way of Cape Sable. They watched both Florida coasts carefully and Lieutenant Hollis and a guard waited two weeks at Cape Sable to intercept them. At 2:30 a.m. on May 17 they arrested seven persons of some importance, but no cabinet member. The most important of the three was Brigadier General Thomas A. Harris, who had been a Congressman from Missouri. With a little more persistence they might have caught Secretary of State Judah P. Benjamin. He had made his way to Bradenton and secured the service of Captain Frederick Tresca to aid his escape. Tresca operated a freight boat from Cedar Key to Key West and during the war had run the blockade to Nassau, using the inside passages that he knew well. Tresca and the fleeing cabinet member stopped at Cape Romano, slaked their thirst with coconut milk, and picked some bananas. They met few humans as they moved southward but those they encountered were friendly. They rounded Cape Sable where the Harris party had been captured two months earlier and secured a heavier boat at Knight's Key for the remainder of the journey to Havana and thence to England.

Occasional passersby left reports of farming activity on the prairie or hammocks behind the Cape. In 1870 a writer in *Harpers Magazine* dismissed as of no consequence farming he saw at Cutler, but "at Cape Sable more thorough and successful experiments have been made in agriculture. Parties in Key West own large tracts and considerable income is derived from the products of these plantations." He wrote also of royal palms at Cape Sable and regretted that so few people would ever see them. It seems unlikely that these were true royal palms, as there is no mention of these after that time and they would most certainly have been mentioned by other visitors. In 1884 A. E. Douglass reported merchants of Key West would "take up" shell islands and get someone to occupy and cultivate them. On East Cape he saw two palmetto houses on the grassy level of the beach and reported that the inhabitants were "no doubt raising early vegetables for the Key West market, but it is not a tempting place for a residence." He also mentioned that vandals had recently cut down the palms that gave Middle Cape its commonly used name of Palm Point. The sentinel palms that marked the point and guided mariners were repeatedly reported as having "recently" been cut down from the time Florida became part of the United States. This story evidently was accepted as true and was passed along over a period of time.

The earliest recorded effort to use the prairie for cattle raising occurred in 1898. Bill Towles and "Doc" Langford of Fort Myers, who grazed many cattle in that area, moved two boatloads of cattle to Cape Sable. They sailed up Little Sable Creek and unloaded the animals to range north of Lake Ingraham. There are also stories of the Raulerson brothers attempting to raise cattle there. The four brothers held preemption grants to the beach as early as 1884 and that portion of the prairie is named for them.

Mrs. Loren Roberts recalls that when she went to Flamingo in 1907 the "Raulerson houses" were standing back on the prairie between Northwest and Middle Cape and that there was a cattle dock at Middle Cape. The buildings had been abandoned but hunting parties sometimes stayed overnight in them. It is quite possible that these early ventures were parts of a combined Towles-Langford-Raulerson operation, with the Raulersons providing the grazing land.

Two explanations are offered for the abandonment of cattle raising. Mosquitoes were probably no worse than in such cattle raising areas as the Caloosahatchee and Peace River valleys, but a plague of mosquitoes and horseflies is commonly blamed. Mosquitoes were so numerous that the nostrils of the cattle

The Waddell Coconut Grove, Cape Sable

became so irritated and swollen that the animals could not breathe. Mosquitoes did make life miserable, but livestock survived at Cape Sable though it did not prosper. The more likely explanation of the situation is that the Cape Sable grass was then, as now, not nutritious enough for cattle grazing.

In March of 1886 Mrs. John R. Gilpin, who was cruising nearby, wrote in her diary:

> We anchor in a sheltered bay south of an east and west stretch of this extreme point of the Florida mainland from Cape Sable to Palm Point. A solitary date palm and a solitary house with doors and windows nailed shut are on this beach of shells. . . . Two solitary pigs prove the existence of some human beings. We find at anchor here a schooner for Key West and two small boats put in for wood. One small boat appeared after the departure of the others, from a point twenty miles up the coast laden with vegetables for Key West. At daybreak sail around the point in a bay above, where a family has settled, and planted a garden of white potatoes, sweet potatoes; started a grove of palm coconuts—they look very yellow and puny. Looks as if the cold had hurt them, but the wife said it was the drought. They are entertaining a taxidermist who had collected a few white herons and roseate spoonbills.

One might speculate that this guest was Jean Chevelier.

Mrs. Gilpin's reference was undoubtedly to the beginnings of

the Waddell Grove, which dominated the Cape Sable waterfront for the next forty years. James A. Waddell of Key West acquired 1,120 acres, originating as preemption claims entered by G. W. Davis, Daniel W. Gallup, Edward Russell, and the four Raulerson brothers; named in the deeds as H.T., J.E., S.H., and S.C., these claims embraced much of the beachfront on the Cape. The lands had not been surveyed but could be preempted under the terms of a law of 1841 which would require the owner of a claim to pay $1.25 an acre when the government surveyed the land preparatory to offering it for public sale. The claims were recorded in 1884 and immediately sold to Waddell. Not until 1903 were they surveyed. Because of the large planting of trees this was sometimes referred to as a "tree claim" after the act of 1872 in which settlers received grants of 160 acres of land for planting forty acres of trees out on the treeless Great Plains in the trans-Mississippi West.

After this time the coconut trees growing down to the waterfront were the outstanding landmark at the Cape, and were always mentioned by visitors. In 1889 the Coast and Geodetic Survey map first records the change of name from Palm Point to Middle Cape—ironically enough, just at a time when coconut palms dominated the scene. The map shows the grove and two buildings, with the trees mostly on Middle Cape but some on East Cape and in between. The 1928 map shows the grove but no buildings; field notes mention houses on East Cape, and we know that the 1935 hurricane destroyed at least one building on Middle Cape.

In 1893 Lieutenant Hugh Willoughby, on his way from Miami around to the mouth of Shark River, anchored early one afternoon on East Cape near a small schooner loaded with wood. He sent a small boat ashore for the schooner's two men to save them from the inconvenience of swimming out to his boat. The following day he passed Middle Cape and referred to the "deserted coconut plantation" and the old house, apparently occupied by a Negro. Nobody else was in sight. Five years earlier Charles A. Dean and party cruising the nearby waters reported many broken down buildings with an Irishman in charge. Another visitor at about the same date reported a fleet of fishing boats at Cape Sable and that he and his three companions laid in a stock of coconuts there.

In 1911 the approximately 8,000 trees (sometimes reported as ten times that many) were reported uncared for, making them appear through glasses to one passing boatman like "shabby gentility." In 1920 Charles Torrey Simpson saw a man sitting on a log who identified himself as the caretaker and said that his nearest neighbor was ten miles away at Flamingo. At that time the two or three houses that had been there previously had been destroyed by a storm.

Captain Tom Annadown purchased coconuts by schooner loads of five thousand in the early thirties at Cape Sable and Long Key. He preferred to buy at Long Key, where they cost him two cents each and where he could engage in other trading as well. Those at Cape Sable cost him as much as five or six cents each. He sold them at Sarasota and St. Petersburg for ten cents each, and if some in the hold of his boat had sprouted they brought as much as a dollar apiece.

The 1925 land boom touched the Cape but lightly. The *Miami Herald* for March 20, 1925 announced that the huge coconut grove would be transformed into a new city at the tip of the United States mainland. The Cape Sable Development Company, capitalized at a million dollars, was to accomplish this miracle. The boom apparently collapsed before the projected development got underway and the land reverted to the

Waddell Estate. Caretakers continued to live there but one suspects that many of them were squatters who took over the buildings for short periods, with or without the knowledge or consent of the owners. In 1933, Allen H. Andrews, reporting in the *American Eagle* on a trip to the Park area with Ernest F. Coe, visited the caretaker at Cape Sable and said that little was left of the coconut grove.

The grove was not a commercial success. Occasionally boatloads of coconuts were taken to market in Miami, but the hopes of the owners were never realized. The caretakers did some farming as well as caring for the grove until the 1935 hurricane swept away the trees, the buildings, and two persons—the daughter and son-in-law of the current caretaker, who was away on vacation. The same storm swept a number of victims from Matecumbe Key into the area. Two unidentified civilians were buried west of Slagle's Ditch. Three unidentified veterans of the CCC camp disaster were found at Christie Point; two of these were cremated and one was buried. A two year old boy was buried at a government work camp on Big Key and five others found on Pan Handle Key were cremated. George Pepper was buried at Madeira Bay. Coincidentally, the body of a Matecumbe woman, Mrs. Buck Grundy, was washed away by the 1960 hurricane and came to rest on Club Key in the same general area. The nearby islands in Florida Bay continued to be occupied although storms usually swept away dwellings and much of the vegetation. By 1947 tarpaper had replaced palm fronds and palmetto leaves for walls and roofs. In 1947, for example, there were five tarpaper shacks on Sandy Key alone.

The final private ownership of the Cape Sable grove lands came in 1945 when Dr. E. C. Lunsford, a Miami dentist, acquired the property and added eighty acres to the original 1,120. Though he was a member of the Everglades National Park board at the time, he apparently thought the Cape lands would not all be included in the Park. He planned a luxury colony, principally for weekenders who would reach the area by boat or airplane until such time as a road to his holdings might be built. He constructed a small landing strip and a cottage on the eastern side of Middle Cape, and a small dock for

A tarpaper shack, Sandy Key, 1947

boats. The decision to include all of the Cape Sable area in the Park and the condemnation of the land for that purpose ended its history of private use and ownership.

Except for the Waddell acreage and the claims of a few squatters around Flamingo the land in the whole area became the property of the Florida East Coast Railway Company in 1912 in settlement of claims for land for railroad construction on the east coast of Florida. The Model Land Company, which managed and sold the lands of the railroad company, planned extensive improvements to drain and open up the area and to attract settlers. They accepted the idea that the land could be drained and that it would be fertile and relatively frost free.

In 1915 they started building a road from Florida City to the Cape, digging beside it the Homestead Canal, which provided fill for the road where it cut through the Everglades as well as drainage. Work was stopped at the Monroe County line until 1922 when the canal-road was extended to Flamingo and from a point two miles north of Flamingo straight west to Bear Lake, where the road now ends. The Homestead Canal, however, continues north of Bear Lake and westward to Gator Lake (to which the road on the canal bank then extended). The canal then continued south to Lake Ingraham and on to the Gulf through a channel cut from the west end of Lake Ingraham. Subsequently a canal was cut into the marl prairie north of the point where the canal entered the big lake. East Cape Canal was dug due south, past the east end of Lake Ingraham, and a side ditch was cut into the lake. Slagle's Ditch and House's Ditch reached up from the bay into East Cape about halfway to the Homestead Canal. Snake Bight Canal east of the road to Flamingo completed the main efforts to drain the Cape Sable prairie and the lands north of it. With specially designed machines, workmen dug many slough ditches in the vain effort to get rid of the excess water. The water connection to Coot Bay which shows on maps was not added until 1945 when Lewis Watson dredged a channel between Coot Bay Pond and Coot Bay for the convenience of boatmen seeking a way into Coot Bay and on into Whitewater Bay.

Lawrence E. Will, who was employed in the digging of the Homestead Canal to Flamingo and Lake Ingraham in 1922, provided an account of the living and construction problems on the project. The dredge was mounted on a barge floating in the canal it was digging. Behind it were barges to house the crew and to bring up supplies, wood, and water. The right of way crew consisted of the Irwin brothers and others from nearby Flamingo. They distilled their drinking water and cut wood and piled it to be picked up as the work progressed. When they reached Bear Lake it was necessary for the water barge, Will's special charge, to go eight miles back up the canal to find fresh water enough to use in the boilers and for cooking purposes, thereby disproving the popular notion that no salt water intrusion existed there until after the region was "drained." A makeshift device on the dredge provided "distilled" water for drinking purposes. The small side ditch to the Fox Lakes was dug by hand to bring fresh water from that source and save the trip to the West Lake area for usable water.

The ditching machines were sometimes abandoned where they had been used, and disappeared only when scrap iron became valuable enough in wartime to make it worthwhile for them to be salvaged. Meanwhile, campers used the sleeping rooms that had been mounted on the dredges for the crews. A big dredge abandoned about ten miles north of Flamingo on the highway was once the site of a whiskey-making operation. Shrimper Bill Brown built a home on the bank of the canal at the north end of Lake Ingraham; the concrete foundations of his shrimp pens remain to mark the site.

The Homestead Canal, before it had been extended beyond the Dade–Monroe county line, induced Frank Irwin to write a letter published in the *Homestead Enterprise* on May 11, 1916. This reflects some of the hopeful thinking that lay behind this and similar drainage projects.

> What we need at Cape Sable is a canal cut from Pine [Long Pine Key] Key deep enough to furnish water in the driest season, bringing it right on through the prairie . . . and out into the bay, so that when the tide which runs out six hours twice in twenty-four would draw a good current of fresh water for stock and irrigation purposes, taking care when getting near the Bay to throw up a good bank on both sides of the canal so that when the tide comes in it would keep the water from backing out of the canal even at high tide. . . . The canal should not touch the bay until it reaches somewhere near Capetown [probably at about East Cape], but it could be made to run out at the Currie Place [at Flamingo]. Then all the land could have laterals [side ditches]. . . . We pay a drainage tax of 5¢ per acre and we don't get any benefit from the Everglades drainage as the Cape is cut off by Whitewater Bay on the north, and on the east by Coot Bay Hammock, and the only drainage that we have is the ditches that have been made by the alligators from Cape Sable Glade into Sable Creek and the rivers that lie north between Whitewater Bay and Cape Sable Glade.

When the Homestead Canal reached Flamingo it was provided with a floodgate that the people living there at the time said "never worked." The canal, like others, solved neither the problem of drainage nor that of fresh water. If the canals let out some excess fresh water in wet seasons, they also let in some salt water in dry seasons.

While its banks of oozy mud slipped into the water in places, especially where it crossed the prairie west of Bear Lake, the Homestead Canal could be navigated by small skiffs and outboards by anyone willing to struggle with overhanging limbs. The Audubon Society cleared a portion of the east end of the canal in 1949 to permit the use of larger boats for wildlife tours. Hurricane Donna in 1960 filled it with debris but dams at the east end of Bear Lake and in East Cape Canal prevented any further use of the waterway. By contrast, all of the narrow and easy-to-bridge ditches cut from the bay into the prairie grew by the washing of the tides into the wide tidal inlets one sees there today. When the Model Land Company sold its land to the government for the Park another effort to combat natural forces in the southern Everglades was written off to experience.

In the early twenties when rum running and alien smuggling were thriving enterprises in South Florida, the possibility of routing these operations by way of the Cape did not escape the attention of enterprising entrepreneurs. Each alien at the time was worth $250 "delivered" in this country. The biggest difficulty was the road—there was only one, and it was uncertain. There was also a serious bottleneck at Homestead where both the Immigration Service and prohibition agents watched the railroad, then extending to Key West, and the highway. The aliens were usually Chinese, but in August of 1924 agents bagged forty Europeans being smuggled in by four Americans. Three years later patrolmen caught seven persons and searched Royal Palm State Park and other likely places before they discovered twenty eight more fugitives. Aliens usually were forced to surrender when a caravan was in any way disrupted since the guides were either caught or escaped, leaving the aliens helpless.

Horace Alderman, one of the largest operators in a combined smuggling and bootlegging operation, wrote an account of his experiences while in the Fort Lauderdale jail awaiting execution for killing some revenue officers while resisting arrest with a cargo of rum. He recalled that the "heat was on" in Miami and a new way of bringing aliens into the area had to be devised. He thought of Cape Sable, and his men made a reconnaissance there. They found the road dry and usable, and a place at Middle Cape where boats could come in close to shore and land the human cargo. So Alderman planned a rendezvous and the signal was given to start. However, it rained and the road became a slippery quagmire. The automobiles could not reach the Cape, and the drivers went ahead to meet the boats and receive the cargo. This done, they started to walk the aliens back to the cars. It was dark and the ruts and potholes were full of water. The mosquitoes were also out in full force.

One old man fell down so many times that he finally could not rise again so he was abandoned. The rest of the group was delayed so long that it was nearly daylight when they reached Homestead, where they fell into the hands of the law.

Some of the most careful explorers of the Park in recent years have been entomologists of the United States Department of Agriculture, popularly known as "cotton pickers." They are engaged in a relentless effort to eradicate tree cotton plants from South Florida. The range of this inoffensive plant on Park lands is along the coastal prairie northward to Marco, and on the Florida Keys is from Key Largo to Key West. Occasional plants have been reported as far north as Melbourne on the east coast and Tarpon Springs on the west coast.

Tree cotton is one of the true cottons, a wild species native to Florida, the Bahamas, Cuba, and the islands to the south. Henry Perrine did not, as is sometimes suggested, introduce it into this country. It is a perennial whose seeds will germinate after lying dormant for as much as fifteen years, making it extremely difficult to eliminate entirely. It may grow to twenty feet or more in height and four inches in diameter, and is sometimes found in dooryards as an ornamental plant. In 1932 pink boll worms, a deadly threat to the field cotton crop of southern United States, were found in the Florida Keys in the bolls of the local tree cotton. The next year the bureau of entomology began an effort to weed out cotton tree plants as a W.P.A. work project. Crews collected and destroyed millions of the wild plants and other thousands in dooryards. At times fifty or more men have been so employed.

Teams of men recruited for the purpose do the "cotton picking" in the winter when rain and mosquitoes interfere less. They first operated from a camp at Flamingo located where the Park Service now has a campground. Their camp is now located a mile farther west on the prairie. Until water for cooking and drinking was made available at Flamingo, it was brought in from a well on the old Jennings Place about ten miles below Paradise Key.

After more than thirty years of effort the hunt continues, giving rise to jests of skeptics that the men must also be planting the cotton. In the watery areas boats are used extensively. Two houseboats with crews of eight men each visit the larger keys and islands. Since tree cotton is not salt tolerant, the mangrove areas washed by ocean water do not have to be examined. The cotton grows luxuriantly on the higher marl lands associated with "sea daisy" or "blue weed" so these are watched for as indicator plants in the eradication surveys. On dry land the areas examined are marked off into sections that are then subdivided into strips by strings, making it certain that every foot of ground is searched. The first crews cut roads throughout the areas over which they traveled in the drier seasons. The road shown on the Coast and Geodetic Survey maps from Flamingo eastward to Crocodile Point, with branches to Porpoise, Shark, and Mosquito Points and westward to East Cape Canal, was built and maintained by these crews. They actually used the old trail to the Northwest Cape area for a time but did not undertake to build and maintain any kind of roadbed. This meant building bridges over some of the canals and ditches, and this also provided a means of easier access to remote areas by hunters, collectors of tree snails and orchids, or the merely curious. Boatmen sometimes found the bridges obstacles to their passage and tore them down. The practice of taking up the planks and leaving only the stringers discouraged travel over these roads and reduced losses of the bridges. The Georgia pine stringers, many of them twelve by eighteen inches and twenty or more feet long, came from the trestles of the Key West extension of the Florida East Coast Railroad. When the 1935 hurricane destroyed the railroad it scattered timbers all over Florida Bay. Some of these were salvaged by the work crews and used in their road making.

In spite of the long history of occupation and use "Down at the Cape," the only buildings left in 1947 when the Park was created were Bill Brown's shrimp house and Dr. Lunsford's small house, landing strip, and dock. After Hurricane Donna swept over the area in 1960 it was almost completely restored to its primitive state.

VII

Flamingo

FLAMINGO lies at the eastern end of the curving Cape Sable prairie, and many local people also used the expression "down at the Cape" when they referred to Flamingo. In former times Flamingo was the only settlement in the entire area; it was centered at the end of the only road from the interior but also encompassed the area westward to East Cape. Flamingo now survives as the southernmost headquarters of Everglades National Park, but the modern development there bears very little resemblance to the original.

The natural features at Flamingo differ from the Cape Sable terrain. There is a protecting fringe of keys out in shallow Florida Bay that is lacking farther west. Conspicuously missing are the sandy beaches so characteristic at the Cape proper; instead the marl prairie reaches down to the water's edge and extends out into the bay in the form of shallow mud flats. Deep water, until a channel was dredged recently, was not available close to shore. As a result, passing boats often landed passengers as far away as Middle Cape where boats could come in closer to shore. The passengers then walked the shoreline or across the prairie to Flamingo.

Like other frontier settlements, Flamingo received its name when the half dozen families living there requested a post office and had to supply a name to identify it. They wanted it named for something characteristic of the area, and easily selected the flamingo as the most distinctive of the many birds that frequented the area. Flamingoes are not native to South Florida, which lies on the outer fringe of their natural range, but they once came in relatively large numbers from Cuba, the Bahama Islands, and possibly other nearby places where they nested. Several hundred were reported at Flamingo in 1902 but rarely any after that time. Later when the presence of the long-legged birds was largely forgotten, at least one writer surmised

Duncan C. Brady (right) *and boat*

that the settlement was so named because the houses were often built on stilts—long flamingo-like legs—to raise them above the level of the flood waters that sometimes swept over the low lying land.

The settlers who established the first post office in 1893 were not the first inhabitants, but the event marked a step toward stability and permanence. The prime mover in the project was Duncan C. Brady. Descended from a New England whaling family, he had never been content to stay in one place very long nor to live very far from the sea. Chance brought him to Savannah, Georgia after a shipwreck, and he never returned north. He married there and moved southward into Florida, working on a towboat in Jacksonville, tending a railroad drawbridge on Lake Monroe, and staying for a while on Merritt Island.

His first trip to the lower peninsula was to bring a load of pineapple slips to Upper Matecumbe Key. He must have liked it (he was plagued by chills and fever from malaria farther north) for he brought his family to Madeira Bay where he cleared a site and built a palmetto shack. He used his sloop, the *Linda C.*, to haul buttonwood and charcoal.

He soon moved to Northwest Cape where the family lived on his boat, there being no house available. He returned to Palm Point, where he found Jim Demery and a family of six children on a farm. He occupied a tenant house on the Waddell place until the caretaker's house became vacant. He moved into that in 1892. The presence of two houses, three horses, and three mules at Palm Point suggests rather extensive farming operations as well as grove caretaking.

Brady found the life of a landlubber too settled for him, and he turned to fishing and woodcutting to supplement the small earnings from freighting. He ferried wood and charcoal to Key West for a village of Negroes who lived at Sawfish Hole, about halfway between Flamingo and East Cape. Just offshore was a favorite turtle set, frequented by people from Key West. The site received its name from the numerous sawfish that got into the turtle nets and ruined them.

When a claim at Flamingo with a small house on stilts became available Brady purchased it, setting the stage for the "founding" of the settlement. He bought a horse to haul wood to the beach, where it was piled for shipping, meanwhile continuing to operate his boat for his Sawfish Hole neighbors. He operated two boats that made weekly trips to Key West. His daughters also recall that they grew enormous squashes and other vegetables, some of which they marketed in Key West.

Once Brady's whaling experience proved useful. Enroute to Flamingo from Key West he discovered a whale aground in a channel near Harvie Key and killed it with an axe. He and some passing sponge fishermen went to work to butcher the whale and fry out the oil. The sharks became so thick that they threatened to carry off the whale before the workers could secure very much of it. Brady's children recall that he sold five hundred dollars worth of oil, but also that someone who arrived to share in the whale oil profits brought whooping cough to the area and all those not previously exposed contracted it.

Brady did not like the low-lying ocean front, fearing a storm might one day destroy his holdings if not his family. He remodeled and enlarged the *Linda C.* and departed in 1894, a few weeks ahead of a storm such as he had feared. He moved to the Chokoloskee Bay and Ten Thousand Islands region and was never again associated with Flamingo.

The newly-christened community showed little signs of growth or even survival. Only scattered accounts give any clue to early activity there. Leverett White Brownell, a visiting naturalist, reported in 1893 that Flamingo was infected with fleas and mosquitoes. He declared that he saw an oil lamp extinguished by a cloud of mosquitoes, that tomatoes were the principal crop and flea powder the staff of life, and that each cabin was thickly sooted by constant use of smudge pots.

Ten years later, and perhaps inspired by the possibility that the Key West extension of the Flagler railroad might be routed that way, all those with land claims in the area—squatters, preemptors, and corporations alike—joined forces to have their lands surveyed. U.S. Deputy Surveyor J. O. Fries came in to run the township and section lines. He prepared a map showing nine "present settlers and their claims." They were C. Dalrymple, N. Nelson, D. J. Bronson, M. Mason, H. R. Fiers, R. D. Vaning, E. Roberts, S. Roberts, and R. M. Weaver.

Flamingo had one resident, Guy Bradley, whose story focused the spotlight of national attention upon the remote hamlet. Edwin R. and Lydia Bradley, with sons Louis and Guy, had settled near Orlando in the 1870's. Edwin Bradley had been a post office employee in Chicago, and later lived at Melbourne and Lantana in Florida. In 1885 the family lived at Lake Worth and the two sons accompanied Charles W. Pierce as far south as Card Sound on the cruise of the *Bonton.* Later that same year the father carried the U.S. mail from Palm Beach to Miami, walking the sandy beach and crossing inlets by skiffs kept there for that purpose. He was also for a time Superintendent of Dade County schools. He became acting superintendent of the Florida Coast Line and Transportation Company, which was dredging a canal on the upper east coast of

Florida. He finally became land agent for the Model Land Company, the land management and sales organization for the railroad, and moved to Flamingo where he and his sons each acquired one quarter mile of waterfront property and where he became postmaster.

Guy Bradley and his brother Louis each had a house at Flamingo when Guy was appointed in 1902 as a county game warden to be paid salary by the Audubon Society. Guy was killed in 1905 protecting a rookery from plume hunters. He was buried at East Cape where a memorial to him was erected.

Only two other persons were known to be buried in the entire region until the victims of the 1935 storm were washed ashore and either cremated or buried there. Tom Alderman's son who died of snake bite and an old man remembered only as Davis, the caretaker of the palm grove, were also buried at East Cape. A gravestone with a hole in it found on Clive

Uncle Steve Roberts at Flamingo

Key was identified as having been picked up elsewhere by a fisherman who bored a hole in it for use as an anchor.

The two Roberts claims at Flamingo belonged to Steve L. Roberts, "Uncle Steve" to all, and his eldest son Eugene. Uncle Steve was locally the best known person to live at Flamingo, and he and his children and grandchildren were closely associated with the area until Flamingo ceased to exist as a place of private residence after the Park was established.

Uncle Steve and his wife, Dora Jane, had lived on a ranch and grove in Orlando until about 1895 when the doctor ordered him to take his wife to the seacoast to live to ward off consumption (tuberculosis), which was prevalent in her family. In 1901 the family went to the upper reaches of Shark River and into Whitewater Bay. One morning they heard the lowing of a cow. Intrigued by the sound, Uncle Steve packed a lunch and started off on foot to investigate. He came out of the woods at Flamingo late in the day, and found half a dozen families there. They invited him to come around and settle, and told him how he could reach there by sailing out of the Shark River and coming around the Cape.

None of the others on the surveyor's list left any record of their lives at Flamingo. They were probably among the many who came and stayed for only a short time, abandoning or selling such claims and dwellings as they had. We know of others who lived there or nearby but who had no official land claims. Robert S. Douthit came with his family from North Carolina to a homestead five miles northwest of Lemon City, now the Little River section of Miami, in 1892, and later made his way to Flamingo. His brother, John E., joined the community a few years later and acquired property there in 1908. Early in the century people remembered include A. P. Curry and a niece, Mrs. Barcus; Dr. E. E. Frear and E. E. McElroy; and Howell Cobb "Judge" Lowe, the local justice of the peace who represented law and order on the coast and lived out toward East Cape. A neighbor and temporary resident was "Governor" W. J. Clark, who had acquired the nickname in Key West when arrested for drunkenness one night. When he appeared in city court the next morning the judge identified himself as the Mayor of Key West and asked the defendant his name.

"Roberts Hotel," Flamingo, rear view

Clark, who lived a few miles north of the city on Stock
Island, responded by identifying himself as "the Governor of
Stock Island."

The Irwins, another family closely associated with Flamingo
for over fifty years, arrived in 1898. Mr. Irwin had been a
brickmaker, and is reported to have been planning to make
bricks there of the local marl, but it seems more likely that he
was attracted by the apparently rich soil for farming and by
the hunting. After he died in 1901, his wife, Sarah Elizabeth,
her son by an earlier marriage, Ray Gooding, and five Irwin
children remained in the area. The four Irwin boys were
Frank, Key, Virgil, and Coleman; the daughter, Carrie, later
married Johnnie Douthit.

Mrs. Irwin and her family homesteaded Joe Kemp Key in 1916; it was known locally as Irwin's Key. She and her family had probably lived there earlier, as they had also lived at several places near Flamingo. Frank Irwin homesteaded Frank's Key in 1921 and lived there with his wife for fourteen months. It had previously been known as Foy Key after a Negro squatter who lived there for many years. Irwin contracted to cut the right-of-way for the completion of the Homestead Canal in 1921 and 1922. He apparently did well on this job for he moved to Homestead and built a house there afterwards.

The other Irwin brothers remained at Flamingo and became commercial fishermen. Coleman built the most substantial house at Flamingo. He gathered heavy timbers for all of the framing and constructed the house eight feet above the ground on pilings that reached through to the roof. After the Park was established this building was used as temporary ranger's quarters and was not removed until it had been damaged by Hurricane Donna.

The Roberts family never lost its connection with Orlando, where they had originated. Two of the sons, Loren and Eugene, married Tanner sisters, Effie and Ada, whom they had known there. When Uncle Steve's wife died in 1923 she was buried in Orlando, and Uncle Steve was visiting there in the home of his daughter, Mrs. Iola Cusak, when he died in 1945.

Uncle Steve reacted to the flurry of interest in Flamingo and the Cape around 1915 by making his home into a hotel. The two story structure had four bedrooms upstairs for regular or transient roomers or boarders. When there was an overflow several mattresses would be put on the floor to accommodate the extra guests. The two story house was destroyed in 1926 by a hurricane and later was rebuilt as a single story structure. Apparently the road to Flamingo had reduced the hotel business to a minimum that no longer required a second floor.

Loren Roberts brought his bride to Flamingo from Orlando in 1907. Mrs. Roberts recalls that the two principal occupations at the time were growing sugar cane and making charcoal. Bob Douthit, Eugene Roberts, and A. P. Curry were the principal cane growers at Flamingo, and Tom Alderman and Judge Lowe several miles toward East Cape. Cane grew on the prairie land down to the water's edge. In the rich soil it grew crop after crop, the cane sprouting up from the stubble when it was cut off, until the 1910 hurricane salted the fields and killed the roots. The farmers then went over to Chatham River and secured seed cane from the Watson Place. Watson himself had been killed just after the storm.

At first only a horse-powered mill was used to grind the cane and extract the juice from which syrup was made in huge kettles. Douthit also ground cane and made syrup for the others. In 1910 Alderman and Lowe purchased a steam engine and a mill for their operations. When their crop was wiped out by the storm they decided to retire from the business and were going to return the mill to Peter Knight, from whom they had purchased it at Key West, but Louis Loudon, who had come to the cane growing community in 1908, and Loren Roberts bought the equipment and set it up at Flamingo, the first and only mill there powered by other than mule or horse and sweep.

The syrup and some of the cane found a market in Key West. While the Key West extension of the Florida East Coast Railway (completed in 1912) was under construction the crews working on it consumed many gallons of Flamingo syrup. But the business, never really large scale, soon died out.

Charcoal making was a long established business in the buttonwood forests around the coast of the lower peninsula. It seems to have been the main reason for settlement at places near Madeira Bay. Crews of Negroes frequently came from Key West and established camps for short periods until they had a boatload of "coal" to take to market. Others, like the Sawfish Hole group for whom Brady freighted, stayed longer. Coal making continued well into the 1930's; Ray Gooding was one of the last of the coal burners. The heap of wood piled for burning but abandoned, pictured on p. 27, was discovered in 1960 on the east bank of the Snake Bight Canal near the outlet.

Coal boats were an important contact with the outside world in the early days at Flamingo. Residents depended upon them to bring food, supplies, mail, and occasional passengers. If a boat was overdue, groceries ran short and residents might be reduced to boiling coconuts for oil to cook game and fish, the only food available. Once Ray Gooding remained away six weeks and came back without any supplies, having spent the money on a spree. His half brothers, the Irwins, joined in chase after him, threatening dire punishment and shooting too close for his comfort.

Allen Chandler came to Redlands in 1904 from Fort Basinger, north of Lake Okeechobee, where he had a small herd of cattle on the open range. He also hunted plume birds, otters, and alligators. He planted an orange grove near his new home but because of his interest in hunting soon found his way to Flamingo. He planted a lime grove there on hammock land near Coot Bay. When his son Luther lost interest in attending high school at fifteen or sixteen years of age, Allen Chandler bought him a boat, which he named the *Belly Ache*. Luther went to Flamingo and stayed there for two years before returning to Homestead to begin a career that made him one of the best known of the pioneer businessmen and growers of the Redlands district. Luther traded the *Belly Ache* for the larger *Estelle* and became the principal boat owner there. He tended his father's lime trees, planted a crop of peppers, and provided boat service for the people at Flamingo who were his father's friends. He lived in the home of Loren Roberts and made ties with Flamingo and its people that were never broken.

Louis Loudon, was from Norwalk, Connecticut originally, and until he reached Flamingo he had suffered from wanderlust. He went first to Panama to work on canal construction; then he decided he wanted to farm so he took passage on a steamer to New Orleans. He went from there to the Imperial Valley in California, but returned to New Orleans and then went on the prospect in Cuba. Finding no place there for someone who spoke only English, he hired off a dock as a mess man to the master of a small boat headed for Miami. There he met Dave Griffin, a Miami policeman who had a small piece of land and a shack at Cape Sable. Griffin must have given Loudon a glowing description of the area because Loudon promptly found passage on a mackerel boat bound from Miami to Punta Gorda, was put off at Middle Cape, and walked across the prairie to Flamingo. Except for a four-year tour of duty in Key West in World War II, he remained at Flamingo until 1949 when he retired to a small home near Florida City.

In 1908 Uncle Steve induced the Crossland Fish Company to build a fish house at Flamingo, which thereafter became increasingly a fishing village. The fish house was on pilings on the edge of the channel. Fishermen used their own boats and Crossland supplied engines and nets. In the fishing season, mid-August to November, a commissary supplied the needs of the fishermen and the fish they caught were credited on their accounts. At the end of the season all of the men went to Miami to settle up. They might have money coming to them or they might be "way in debt." When the season was over the commissary service ended and the families salted fish, hunted, or cut wood for their living, sending the coal boats to Key West for their supplies.

Several attempts to operate a school at Flamingo met with indifferent success. Girls sent from Key West as teachers didn't stay long. When residents discovered that Arthur Frye, a bachelor living in a shack back on the prairie, knew the rudiments of the basic classroom disciplines they pressed him into service as a teacher, as they did Mrs. Eugene Roberts for a time also. One suspects the boys and girls were none too eager pupils. In 1921 Loren Roberts, like many others, moved his family to Florida City so that his children could attend school. His family never cut ties with Flamingo, however, and in 1939 he began operating the most successful fish house ever there.

Once on the annual trip to Miami Loren Roberts brought

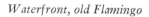

Waterfront, old Flamingo

back a milk cow on the runboat. He built a screened stall to protect the animal at night. By mid-morning there was usually a breeze and the cow could be turned out to graze and not be bothered too much by the mosquitoes and flies, but before evening it soon learned to head for its stall. A member of the family always opened the stall door quickly to prevent letting in too many insects, just as they did in their home. Mrs. Roberts remembers wearing a netted hat and heavy blue denim clothes and carrying a smudge to keep the insects away when she entered the stall to milk the cow. It is said that chickens, too, learned when it was safe to be abroad.

Except when Dr. Rufus C. McGahey, a retired physician from Tennessee, was homesteading a key in Florida Bay from 1912–1917 there was no professional medical care at Flamingo. On rare occasions mothers went to nearby towns to give birth, but the services of a midwife were used by most; these were performed by Dora Jane Roberts as long as she lived. There were no religious services unless an itinerant preacher happened by and held services in one of the homes.

Flamingo grew scarcely at all. At times it lost population but it was never abandoned. The completion of the railroad across the Florida Keys brought civilization closer but altered life little. The stations along the Keys lacked docking facilities and the offerings of the small stores there were limited. Islamorada was made the post office for the Flamingo area in 1914. A. P. Curry had previously acted as postmaster and also kept a small store—said to be the only one in Flamingo history—but abandoned both jobs in 1909. For several years afterwards the mail, when it came at all, was distributed at the home of Loren Roberts in the old Guy Bradley house. Residents continued to depend mainly on coal boats, fish boats, and later on fish trucks to bring in their supplies.

In 1920 Charles Torrey Simpson reported only a few houses at the little settlement of Flamingo, and two or three abandoned shacks on nearby hammock land. Occasionally a schooner would load buttonwood for the Key West market, "these being the only signs of life one ever meets in this lonely region." Lawrence E. Will visited Flamingo in 1922 and described it as having only three houses, with one at East Cape and one at Middle Cape.

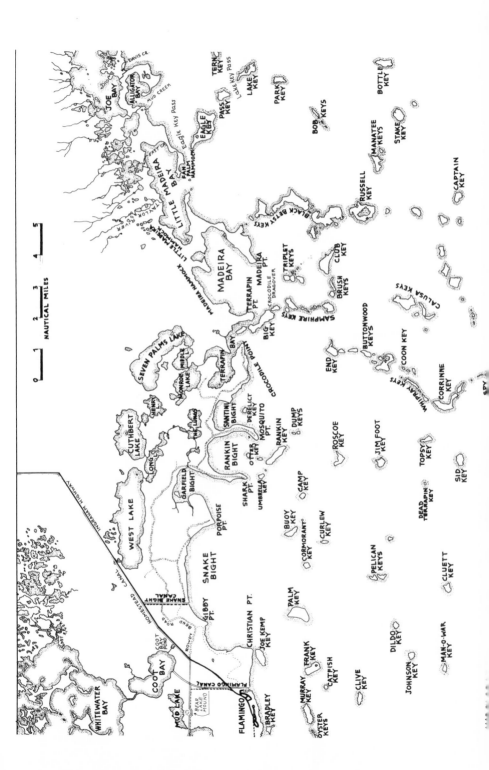

He was told there had been more residents earlier. Mrs. Loren Roberts thinks there may have been fewer residents when she moved away in 1921 than in 1907 when she arrived.

The isolation, difficulty of access by water, lack of any road to the interior, limited living area and economic promise, danger of storm damage, and the constant plague of insects were enough reasons to account for Flamingo's lack of growth. Anyone who ever lived there or visited there in the rainy season retains vivid recollections of the mosquitoes. All writers mention them and some have let their imaginations run wild.

Herbert K. Job, an ornithologist, visited Flamingo in 1903. He described it as inhabited by a handful of settlers who had taken up government claims along the shore, "cleared a few openings in the mangroves, and built their crude cottage or curious palmetto shacks." Two guides, one of them Guy Bradley, accompanied him on his field trips to, among other places, Cuthbert Rookery. This rookery was named for the first plume hunter who made his way to it and reaped its rich harvest of valuable feathers. Job said the birds were wonderful to behold but he was impressed most by the mosquitoes. The land was fertile, but he said lack of fresh water together with the mosquitoes made it a near impossible place to live. Homeowners, he wrote, kept a bunch of palmetto leaves hanging outside the door for those about to enter to knock off the mosquitoes before coming inside. Others kept a smudge of black mangrove and lived eternally in smoke. He invented the unlikely story of seeing mothers wheel their babies with a smudge burning under the carriage as they went to a religious service in a building used both as a schoolhouse and church. Inside the building he said smudges burned, the congregation slapped mosquitoes, and the children chased horseflies, appropriately called "sharpshooters" by the natives.

One story had a United States health officer explaining to a resident that Uncle Sam had means to kill 95 per cent of the pests. The Flamingoite, to the amazement of the outlander, was unimpressed and finally simply said, "You wouldn't miss 'em." Perhaps Flamingo should also be credited with the statement that one could make a swing with a pint cup and catch a quart of mosquitoes.

Stephen Cochran Singleton of Key West, writing in the *Homestead Leader* of June 19, 1928, reported an idea he had found in a book. Bat towers might solve the problem of mosquitoes on the Florida Keys and eradication could be accomplished in a couple of years at a dollar an acre cost. He commented, "We are satisfied the bats will not starve for some time at any rate." Shortly afterwards in 1929 a bat tower was constructed on Sugarloaf Key at a settlement then known as Perky. It was constructed for B. C. Perky, who owned a fishing camp on the island, and was complete with bat roosts and metal rat guards. Dr. Charles A. R. Campbell, city bacteriologist for San Antonio, Texas provided the specifications for the tower, and when it was completed he sold Perky his special bat bait for $500. The smelly bait failed to attract any of the few bats in the area and a hurricane several months later washed the bait away. The tower still stands uninhabited. When Perky tried to reorder the bait he found that Dr. Campbell's secret formula had died with him. At about the same time an abandoned utility building at the crossroads on Marco Island became a favorite haunt for bats but nobody there ever suggested that they had any effect on the local mosquito population.

Hope never died that Flamingo might some day come into its own. This dream was shared by residents and developers alike. The Model Land Company built a road from Florida City through Paradise Key, headed eventually for Flamingo. In 1916 they advertised land in Homestead and Cape Sable, referring to the coming road as the greatest in Florida. They predicted the Cape would have the earliest and the best fruits and vegetables. Sugar cane twelve to fifteen feet high, its juice producing thirty per cent syrup or sugar, was promised. In March, 1915, Port Sable Townsite was announced by W. R. Burton of Redland in the *South Florida Banner*. He had 65 acres of bay front land which he had plotted in lots and put on the market at prices ranging from twenty to fifty dollars. He offered land free to anyone who would build a hotel.

The spring number of the *Tropic Magazine* in 1917 announced the incorporation of the Pioneer Plantation Company to plant 3,000 acres of Cape Sable land to staple crops. This may refer to lands around Paradise Key, where many acres were planted in tomatoes after the road to Florida City was opened. Oddly enough, not only was water harder to control but temperatures were lower rather than higher and the danger of frost greater south of Paradise Key. The *Homestead Enterprise* reported on September 20 of the same year that a dehydrating plant was soon to be erected at Cape Sable. Chicago capitalists, it said, were planning to carry on the business of dry preserving vegetables on a large scale. The plant at Cape Sable was to be ready by February and another at Homestead the next year. The investors planned to put up the buildings in Chicago and then dismantle and ship them to Cape Sable.

About this same time S. B. Jennings planted 300 acres of young orange trees on the abandoned portion of Ingraham Highway below Paradise Key, down toward Flamingo, and established a home there with a double row of royal palms flanking the drive up to the house. The grove was laid out somewhat like a modern vegetable farm on the low lands, with ditches and dikes for water control. But this was not good citrus land. The home was occupied until the 1926 hurricane damaged both it and the grove. Local people used oranges from the grove for a time but by 1940 the driveway and some palms were the only remains of the Jennings venture.

In 1921 when the road to Flamingo neared completion it was reported unofficially that surveys had been made for an extension of the railroad to Cape Sable. When the road reached the settlement in 1922 it made little if any difference at first, and the railroad link never materialized. The last five miles of the road were scarcely navigable in wet weather; after a shower it became slick and slippery. One driver of a small flatbed truck carrying a few crates of tomatoes recalls that only a small tree kept him and the truck from falling into the roadside canal but that the tomatoes did slide into the water. Many an early sports fisherman had the experience of going in on a dry road and returning after a shower when it required the efforts of an entire party to keep a car on the road and headed in the right direction. When the road became really saturated it was an apparently bottomless bog. Fish and other produce were then floated on

Last mile, Flamingo Road, about 1946

lighters up the canal beyond the most treacherous stretch and transferred there to trucks.

Asked what difference the road made, Louis Loudon replied laconically, "None. There were fewer people than ever at Flamingo. They had found a way to get out." The road was not much improved until the National Park Service put a gravel top on it to make it usable while the modern road now in use was constructed.

Fish did not begin to be taken out by road until 1939 when the Crossland Fish Company terminated the runboat service. Loren Roberts then successfully operated a fish house and trucked fish out. Drivers often piled slabs of limestone rock in the trucks on the return trips and dropped them into the worst mudholes in a vain effort to build up some "bottom." Some portions were covered with tree trunks laid side by side across the road to make a stretch of "corduroy" surface.

Fishing increased at Flamingo and in 1947 two other fish houses were operating, both using trucks, in addition to the Roberts establishment. Lloyd "Barrelhead" House had started his operation in 1943, and Charles Andrews his in 1945. The three fish houses employed fifty to seventy five more or less transient fishermen besides the long time residents who also fished for their livelihoods.

Fish trucks became the contact with the outside world. The Roberts trucks left orders for household supplies and food at his home in Florida City, and picked up the goods on a return trip the next day. Mrs. Roberts kept accounts of the orders and they were later charged against the fishermen's credits entered in the books of the fish houses at Flamingo. The effort to restore runboat service after the Park road was closed to commercial vehicles did not prove successful.

Some of the Flamingoites had automobiles but the majority of the fishermen had none. Car travel was often limited by wet roads. The first automobile was brought to Flamingo in 1917 by Dr. Herman Slagle, a retired dentist who had a real es-

Flamingo from the air, about 1947

tate development near East Cape on land now marked by Slagle's Ditch and the foundation of a clubhouse the Model
Land Company had built there. The clubhouse was a long
structure with a hallway down the center and five rooms on
each side. Meals were served on a screened porch that ran
the length of the building on the east side. Dr. Slagle's automobile was brought in by boat, as were the patrons of the hostel-
ry, real estate prospects, hunters, and fishermen. Boats brought
visitors from points on the Keys railroad extension or from
places like Miami to a dock on the beach where the clubhouse
stood on stilts. The automobile was used to take people over
the open prairie if it was dry. Later A. R. Livingston, a surveyor and civil engineer long associated with the area, bought
a Chalmers automobile that he later sold to Loren Roberts.
Mrs. Roberts recalls that they could take rides down the beach
in dry weather. At least one person who visited the clubhouse,
William Burdine of Miami, liked Flamingo well enough to
remain associated with it long after the clubhouse was forgotten.

In spite of the clubhouse, the drainage ditches, and other
efforts, real estate at Flamingo could not compete with the
more accessible and attractive lands being opened up at the
same time by drainage and reclamation in areas like Lake
Okeechobee and the east coast from Miami northward. Flamingo became almost exclusively a commercial fishing village, with
sports fishermen and hunters there in season in small numbers.
Alligator and plume bird hunting were no longer legal and
the law could now reach offenders easily. Charcoal making
had ceased and farming was limited to that for local use. There
had been a flurry of farming activity after the road came;
several people homesteaded on nearby keys and the records show
a surprising number of mortgages to fertilizer companies. However, these enterprises did not last.

Farmers were occasionally employed by vegetable brokers in
Florida City and Homestead, but the activity reached no large
proportions. Mike Santanello, now a Coral Gables paint manu-
facturer and distributor, recalls coming down from Philadelphia in 1930 in the midst of the depression and taking a job
at two dollars a day to work at growing tomatoes and peppers

on land between Flamingo and Bear Lake. He lived in a tin shack and cooked out of doors on a stove made of stones. He recalls the hunting with special pleasure.

The 1935 hurricane did extensive damage in the Flamingo area and salted the land, killing all growing crops. Rains leached out the salt almost immediately but farming had already run its course. That small-scale industry lost out to the more accessible, more easily drained, and irrigated lands opening up in the interior of the peninsula.

The road opened the way to another activity that took on new importance. Moonshiners had always supplied the needs of the local community for whiskey. The local product, "Cape Sable Augerdent," was a fearsomely powerful brew never forgotten by the uninitiated after the first drink. Van Campen Heilner visited Flamingo about 1919. He reported that quite a crowd came out to his boat, the *Nepenthe*. He played the phonograph for them and "did the vanishing act with a pint of corn whiskey and retired in somewhat of a stupor. . . . I thought I had been drinking carbolic acid." On another occasion a Miamian who knew the qualities of the product was offered a drink from a wine bottle. He accepted, thinking that it was actually wine. He withstood the shock of discovery that it was potent Augerdent but was unable to warn his companion, who took a swig and was so visibly shaken that tears streamed down his cheeks.

Bootleggers could now reach the urban market as far away as Miami. The necessity to drive through Florida City was a threat to successful evasion of the law, but bootleggers were not sought after as zealously as were alien smugglers. A secondary outlet by way of U.S. Highway 1 was sometimes used when pressure was too strong at Florida City and Homestead. Bootleggers followed a boat trail from the Flamingo road near Whiskey Creek through the inner fringe of mangroves to Little Madeira Bay, and then along the coast and inland ponds to a Manatee Creek landing, where the cargo could be transferred either to a waiting car or truck or even to a larger boat. The center of whiskey making was about ten miles north of Flamingo along the creeks and channels that led east and west from the highway. Along Whiskey Creek east and west of the road one may still see the remains of abandoned furnaces and stills ruined by prohibition agents twenty or more years ago.

Other moonshiners had their "landings" scarcely concealed by the mangrove bushes growing on the roadside on the east side, from which they could load and unload skiffs or barges. Recently the writer went by canoe to Noble's Hammock where a boardwalk made of barrel staves laid across parallel cypress timbers led from a small dock out to the still. The remains of a brick furnace and some metal gashed by the ax blows of an enforcement officer indicate the nature of the operation, which is given added importance by the discovery of an eight-inch well some ten feet deep that presumably supplied fresh water during wet periods. Many of these buttonwood hammocks had pools of fresh water during rainy periods; these became brackish in dry weather.

Asked what they used for fuel, a long time resident replied buttonwood. Didn't the smoke reveal the hiding place? "Oh no," he replied, "There were so many cooking fires everywhere that nobody paid any attention to them." But enforcement became more effective and even the most ingeniously contrived operations were sooner or later discovered, dispelling any notion of immunity that they might have cherished. Many Flamingo residents, who had lived so long in freedom and isolation, would not or could not believe that game laws applied to them or that society forbade unlicensed individuals to make and sell intoxicants tax-free.

There were also some settlements around the coast east of Flamingo. A cistern, eight by twelve feet on the sides and twenty-four inches deep, on Christian Point marks a now forgotten home site. Sometime about 1940 the E. T. Knight Fish Company established a base near the mouth of Snake Bight Canal from which the road alongside the canal joined the one to Flamingo. The fish house was on the west side and the fishermen's huts on both sides; remains of these may still be seen. Unlike the fishermen at Flamingo, all of whom used inboard and outboard skiffs or larger craft, the men at Knight's fish house used airboats, fishing the inland waters which often had to be reached by moving over shallow flats. Sports fishermen in

E. C. Knight Fish Company, Snake Bight

propeller-driven craft were often rescued from the mud flats by some of these shallow-draft fishermen.

On Gibby's Point beyond Snake Bight a Negro by the same name established himself to make charcoal from nearby buttonwood. He had a modern still used, he said, to distill fresh water for his personal use, but unconvinced revenue officers destroyed it as a whiskey making plant.

Interest in Madeira Bay and the mahogany growing there antedates any recorded activity at Flamingo, and it was undoubtedly more important at one time than the fishing village. Duncan Brady stopped there in the early nineties. Adolphus Santini's diary records that Mr. Youmans and his wife moved to Madeira Bay in 1893. Ted Smallwood, who had come to Chokoloskee several years earlier, moved to Madeira for a time and also spent a season at Miami before he married and settled down to spend the remainder of his life at Chokoloskee. Building sites may be seen on Davis Creek, named for Raoul Davis, a crocodile hunter and farmer, Mud Creek, East Creek, Taylor Creek, and on the northeast corner of Little Madeira Bay on the north side of an indentation in the shore there. There was once a one-room house on stilts at the end of Seven Palms Lake, where seven royal palms stood in a row as if they had been planted. These trees all died after being damaged by the 1935 hurricane except for one killed by Hurricane Donna in 1960. The extent of the interest in the region at an early date may be indicated by a map of Madeira dated June 14, 1895 in which it is laid out in 121 lots. Since there is no dedication on the plot, it may never have passed beyond that stage. Whatever the dreamer or planner had in mind, Madeira was never to have great importance in the twentieth century. Its waters were too shallow, the land near its shores too low, the fine stand of mahogany gone, buttonwood, its only other resource, lost its value as a fuel, and no stream provided access to the interior.

Coot Bay was an important center of activity for a time. In the buttonwood hammocks south of the bay there was considerable charcoal making and farming. A house built on pilings about six feet above the ground stood just off the Bear Lake Road (about halfway out to the lake) until Hurricane Donna turned it over. But the bay itself was more important. Its waters provided easy access to the interior and the Gulf coast by way of Whitewater Bay and Shark River. A road or trail marked the way to Flamingo. When the Homestead Canal was cut across it in 1922 it was bridged just west of the Flamingo branch where the road followed the canal bank southward. At the end of the road on Coot Bay a dozen small boats might be tied up at the docks there at that time. Captain Louis Watson was based there until he cut the passage into Coot Bay Pond in 1945. He operated there from a dock at the roadside. The National Park Service also maintained a ranger station there until the new road and facilities were constructed at Flamingo.

Coot Bay remains famous for the number of coots and ducks that visited it in season, and was once a popular place for hunters to gather. For some years a houseboat stationed there provided food and drink for hunters and other occasional visitors. The remains may still be seen where it burned down to the water line. Coots were prized principally for their large gizzards and many visitors recall the dish of rice and coot gizzards in which one camp specialized.

No amount of romantic and sentimental recollections can bring back "the good old days" at Flamingo or any other part of the Park. They were in fact gone or rapidly disappearing before the dedication of the Park in 1947. Nor can the creation of a national park restore all that once attracted people; it can only preserve what remains of it and make it accessible to people who come to see and appreciate it. Old Flamingo was the single instance of a community stronger in 1947 than it had been earlier and it is safe to speculate that its future would have been changed radically had there been no Park. Any continuing occupation and development would have required road-building, dredging channels, reclaiming land, and other development probably not unlike that which has followed at modern Flamingo.

The new Flamingo is in as sharp contrast to the Park itself as to the old Flamingo. A modern marina with launching ramps, boat livery, and supplies; a visitors' center and museum; a ranger station and housing for Park and other personnel; motel and restaurant accommodations; and charter boats for fishing and sightseeing cater to the comforts and needs of people who come to visit one of the country's last unique wildernesses. Outside this modern community every effort is being made to restore and maintain the state of nature that existed there before the first pioneers visited the lower end of the Florida peninsula.

VIII   The Park—Idea to Realization

THE PARK IDEA, as distinguished from the organized effort to secure its establishment, was at least half a century older than its achievement. Some of the first naturalists who visited the region and exclaimed over its relatively untouched and tremendously valuable assets undoubtedly dreamed of protecting the area from exploitation. Early reports and recommendations, the later frontal attack by the prime mover of the organized planners, Ernest F. Coe, and some of the present plans and problems are presented here for those who not only wish to know how so much land was set aside to create Everglades National Park, but who may also wish to join the group of dedicated persons who must be constantly vigilant to preserve and protect what now belongs to all.

The conservation movement was not unique to South Florida. The turn of the century witnessed a new awareness of the possibility that unrestrained use of America's natural resources might strip the land of its rich inheritance. The first president to take note of this current of opinion, Theodore Roosevelt, lent enthusiastic support to the idea of creating national parks for this purpose.

The idea was not easily achieved. The aims sounded good in principle but ran contrary to long-established practice. Perhaps more importantly, the conflicts with already-established vested interests proved, here as elsewhere, almost unsurmountable.

In Florida in the proposed Park area lumbermen were cutting cypress, pine, and mahogany. Canneries were stripping the clam beds in the Ten Thousand Islands, and commercial fishermen were depleting certain species of fish. Game hunters were burning off and shooting out one of the last heavily populated wildlife areas in the country, and plume hunters had long since endangered the survival of some of Florida's most beautiful birds. Collectors were taking away valuable rare species of plants and animals. Real estate developers were planning land reclamation and settlement. Oil prospectors suggested that the area contained oil-bearing lands of commercial importance. Public and private lands were largely under lease, and counties lamented the loss of potential land tax revenues.

Outside of the Park area cattle ranching was expanding, and vegetable growing and farming were spreading as land was drained and irrigated. Fresh water sources of the lower Everglades were being tapped for commercial use or diverted to further upset the balance of nature, vitally affecting the Park region and increasing the danger of devastation by fire.

Everyone felt conservation was commendable except where it directly affected his own economic interests. One may well wonder how the Everglades National Park was finally achieved.

The Park idea did open up some promises of investment, development, and profit. To the people of a state where tourism was beginning to count so heavily in the economy, the promise of a million visitors a year was an enormous asset and a new drawing card. Recent estimates of income derived reached tens of millions of dollars annually. This potential certainly helped to swing the balance in favor of the creation of a national park in South Florida.

The discovery of the biological treasures of Paradise Key in 1893 focused attention on the magnificent stand of royal palms there. Dr. H. P. Rolfs, Dean of the University of Florida College of Agriculture and later Director of the Florida Agricultural Experiment Station, together with Dr. N. L. Britton, Director of the New York Botanical Garden, came to examine the palms. Since the weather was quite dry they decided on an overland trip rather than going by boat as the discoverers had ten years earlier. Rolfs and Britton started from Cutler by carriage. The road was good as far as Captain Haden's place, after which it became little more than a trail. At Homestead where they expected to find a commissary they found only a watchman guarding tools for the Florida East Coast Railway Company. At Florida City they left the railroad right-of-way and, following the old surveyor's trail, reached their destination on the third day. Dr. Rolfs later reported that Paradise

Key later came near to becoming a park as a result of that trip. When he showed photographs of the royal palms to Dr. A. F. Woods the instant reply was, "That must be preserved as a national park."

President Roosevelt was empowered by an Act of Congress to accept gifts of such areas for the nation. Assuming that the land belonged to the Florida East Coast Railroad, Rolfs and Britton took up the matter with Frederick I. Morse, local agent of the railroad, who referred them to J. E. Ingraham, a vice president of the company. Ingraham, who had made a journey across the upper Glades from Fort Myers to Miami in 1892, was willing to grant the land. However, the eastern end of Paradise Key was not the property of the carrier and the only person having the authority to sell the land, the agent of the owner, was absent in Europe. Before negotiations could be pursued any further, the president's authority to accept such grants lapsed and was not later renewed.

Though they made no specific proposal for a park, Edwin A. Dix and John M. McGonigle implied as much in an article in *Century Magazine* of February, 1905, when they compared the Florida Everglades with other natural wonders. They wrote, in part, "Their mystery is a part of our national inheritance. . . . It has its place among the Country's native wonders like the Mammoth Cave and Niagara Falls. . . . After all, it is rather a good thing to have a little of wonderland left."

Another early writer who supported the Park idea and whose work was widely circulated was A. W. Dimock, who wrote enthusiastically in *Florida Enchantments*:

> Within my own recollection of the West Coast of Florida, alligators slept on the banks of every river, great white and blue wading birds stalked across every flat, solid areas of waterfowl covered the bays and streams, the trees were burdened and the skies darkened by great flocks of birds of georgous plumage and by others of purest white, the most beautiful of created creatures.
>
> There is just one power that can bring back the power of that lotus land: restock its waters and people its forests again for the education and enjoyment of the whole people to whom it belongs. That power is active public sentiment. . . .
>
> The networks of rivers, chains of lakes, beautiful Everglades

and ten times Ten Thousands Islands of South Florida will be all the year playgrounds of the coming generation. Their most conspicuous charm, which has departed might be restored if the birds of Florida could secure the same protection as the beasts of the Yellowstone National Park.

The noted ornithologist Frank M. Chapman, after four attempts, finally succeeded in making the trip to the Cuthbert Lake rookery in 1908. Audubon warden Guy Bradley, killed in 1905, had stopped one of Chapman's efforts when he told him it had already been shot out. In late March of 1908 Guy's brother Louis Bradley and Melch Roberts guided Chapman, A. C. Bent, famous for his scholarly life histories of North American birds, and Louis Agassiz Fuertes, renowned painter and naturalist, to the famed rookery. Writing about this experience in *Camp and Cruises of an Ornithologist* Chapman commented, "Cuthbert Rookery should be preserved both because it is fine example of a type of communal bird life for which Florida was once distinguished and because it will be the last refuge for several species of birds, which, without such protection, will shortly become extinct in the United States." He estimated it would require two wardens for four months each year in the nesting season to adequately protect the birds.

Related movements elsewhere added strength to the aim of preserving the unique flora and fauna of the Park region. One of the first and most influential was the effort of the National Association of Audubon Societies (now the National Audubon Society) to protect the fast-vanishing bird life in Florida. In May, 1901, William Dutcher, president of that group and also chairman of the Committee on Bird Protection of the American Ornithological Union, came to Tallahassee and secured in the state legislature the introduction and passage of a model non-game bird protection law. However, means were not available to enforce the statute. There was only one game warden for each county, and the Monroe County officer had the impossible task of dividing his attention between the area from Key West to Key Largo and across Florida Bay to the lower point of the mainland. To implement enforcement of the new law, the Audubon Societies employed at their own expense four wardens to watch the rookeries in the state. Guy Bradley was assigned to the Park area.

Bradley's death in 1905 in pursuit of his commission to prevent the slaughter of the newly-protected birds gave the cause a martyr, and his sponsors called national attention to the conservation problem involved. The murder of Warden C. G. McLeod in the same service near Charlotte Harbor three years later added fuel to the burning zeal of the protectors of birds.

Events far removed from the Florida Everglades also operated to protect its bird life. T. Gilbert Pearson, then Executive Secretary of the Audubon Societies, successfully sponsored a controversial bill in the New York legislature to outlaw the commercial use of American wild bird feathers in that state. Since New York was the center of designing and manufacturing American millinery, this was close to a death blow for the use of feathers in that industry. Governor Charles Evans Hughes signed the bill into law in 1910. The legal battle was not fully won, however, as Florida feather hunters sold their wares to agents for foreign buyers, who then shipped them back into New York. It required a tariff barrier to stop this importation. Finally changes in hat styles and an aroused public conscience made the wearing of feathers unpopular if not illegal.

In December, 1930, T. Gilbert Pearson, then president of the Audubon organization, testified before the Public Lands Committee of the United States Senate that impostors masquerading as Audubon wardens were watching colonies of egrets until they were "ripe" and then shooting them out. Further, local people had reported for years that Cuban fishermen coming to the coast to catch mackerel would, at the end of the season, go up Shark River, shoot birds by the thousand, salt them down, and take them back to Havana. It was also charged that local hunters killed birds in the same fashion and bootlegged them in Key West. A rookery found shot out in 1937 substantiated these charges. Clearly the Audubon groups needed assistance in their campaign to protect the plume birds.

Botanist John Kunkel Small, who came to Florida first in 1902 to collect plant specimens for the New York Botanical

Garden, was a strong supporter of the Park idea. In 1916 he was quoted as agreeing with David M. Fairchild, whose tropical plant introductions into South Florida are today recognized world wide by Fairchild Tropical Garden in Coconut Grove, that many of the smaller hammocks should be owned by the government because of the rare growth found in them. In 1937 in a letter to Dr. Fairchild, Dr. Small recalled that the outstanding and little known unique character of the flora and fauna had impressed him from the first. "The whole natural ensemble," he wrote, "was so different from that of any other within our country that agitation was at once started to have at least a part of that region set aside for the benefit of posterity."

Dr. Small again came to the support of the Park idea when he wrote in *Eden to Sahara*:

> Here is a unique El Dorado, mainly a tongue of land extending hundreds of miles into tepid waters reaching almost to the Tropic of Cancer, where the floristics of temperature, subtropic and tropic regions not only meet, but mingle, where the animals of temperate regions associate with those of the tropics . . . . as much as possible of this natural history museum should be preserved, not only for its beauty, but also for its educational value, for it is within easy reach of the majority of the population of the United States. Steps for protection of selected areas should be taken at once by the state and federal governments. . . .

Ales Hrdlicka, an anthropologist who visited the southwest coast of the peninsula in 1918, made a survey of Indian mounds there. In his book *Anthropology of Florida*, commenting on the Turner River shell mounds, he wrote, "The site is so characteristic, so easily approached and probably so important to science that steps, it would seem, ought to be taken to preserve it for posterity which could best be done by making it a national reservation."

Naturalist Charles Torrey Simpson, writing about the Cuthbert Lake region in *In Lower Florida Wilds*, urged that the area be included in a national park. Visiting the proposed Park area as much as twice a year for thirty years, he never ceased his advocacy of a means to preserve remnants of the wildlife he saw disappearing so rapidly.

Editor Allen H. Andrews in an editorial on January 16, 1923 in the *American Eagle,* published by the Koreshan colony at Estero, Florida, and writing about the dedication of another park, asked the question, "Why not a great National Park for Florida?" He devoted much space in the *Eagle* to horticultural topics, several times visited the Park area, and gave the idea unqualified endorsement.

Also in 1923, Director of the National Park Service, Stephen T. Mather, in a report to the Secretary of the Interior, stated, "There should be an untouched example of the Everglades of Florida established as a national park." The desirability seems to have come to official attention at least as early as 1920.

Interest in Paradise Key continued. Dr. Small was one of the most frequent and concerned visitors. In 1909 he reported that he had met a group of six or eight men going in to prospect. They proposed to acquire land and plant citrus. The construction of a rough road along the route of the old surveyor's trail increased the number of visitors and the threat to the biological treasure trove.

The Florida Federation of Women's Clubs came to the rescue of Paradise Key. In 1910 J. E. Ingraham told Mrs. Kirk Munroe, then chairman of the Federation, about Paradise Key and she suggested it be given to her organization. On December 28, 1914, a delegation of Federation ladies accompanied by former Governor William S. Jennings and D. Bryan Jennings visited the site. By this time a road had been built through the hammock by the Model Land Company. Mrs. William J. Krome of Homestead, a member of the party, suggested that the road be named Ingraham Highway. Governor and Mrs. Jennings endorsed the suggestion and the Dade County Commissioners approved the name.

The dedication of Royal Palm State Park took place on November 22, 1916; 150 automobiles brought 750 people to the event. The railroad company, which owned alternate sections of land in the region, donated 640 acres of land. When the state of Florida in 1915 contributed 960 acres, the railroad increased its gift to the same amount. In 1921 the state added 2,080 acres of surrounding land, primarily to help maintain the original tract.

The Federation hoped to make the new park a self-supporting project. They planned a lodge where visitors might be housed and fed. They invited gifts and rented the land adjacent to Paradise Key to tomato farmers. Charles A. Mosier became the first caretaker on March 1, 1916. When his daughter returned to visit in July, 1959, she recalled that the family had lived in a tent until 1919 when the lodge was completed. The tent had a wooden floor and was screened. Under the direction of Mosier and his successors, the Federation laid out paths through the hammock, constructed a small deer pen, and gradually added to the facilities. Much of the original fencing of the deer pen is still intact.

The financial hopes of the Federation were not realized. None of the sources of revenue came up to expectations, and

Lodge, Royal Palm State Park

disastrous fires repeatedly threatened all of the vegetation on Paradise Key. Lodge rentals in 1923 totaled only $821.76 and a fish-bowl collection allocated for fire protection netted only $214.40. The 1926 hurricane followed by fires in 1927 led the Florida legislature to aid the cause with $10,000 appropriated for a two-year period for restoration, and a subsequent annual appropriation of $2,500 for maintenance. Fire had destroyed the jungle on the north side of the highway. New trails needed to be opened on the south side. Two pumping engines and a number of fire wells were installed. In 1932 the Homestead Fire Department came to help bring a fire in the same area under control.

In 1934 Royal Palm State Park was declared a conservation area and was thereby entitled to federal assistance. Civilian Conservation Corps workers were assigned there from November of 1934 to June, 1935. These youthful victims of the depression widened, beautified, and graveled the trails, built a rest shelter, and planted 541 royal palms. They extended the deer pen to include five acres and built a rock feeding shelter at the entrance to the pen. They replaced the storm-wrecked garage with a native stone structure, built a powerhouse of the same rock, and sawed hundreds of fallen trees into firewood. Improvements to buildings included the addition of a porch to the servants' quarters, a bathroom at the rear of the lodge, and general repairs to buildings. All of these buildings have now been torn down except the concrete and rock pump house.

At the annual meeting of the Federation in Daytona Beach in 1929, upon the recommendation of Mrs. W. S. Jennings, the chairman of the Royal Palm State Park Committee, the Federation formally offered the park they had maintained since its creation thirteen years earlier to the proposed national park if and when it should be created. Appropriately enough, the first visitors' center of Everglades National Park was established at Paradise Key, the heart of the state park.

Organized activity that led directly to the establishment of Everglades National Park began in the 1920's. In 1922 a small group met in the real estate offices of Fulford by the Sea and subsequently founded the Florida Society of Natural History. Those present, like many others, were concerned about reports of careless use and wanton destruction of the natural resources in Florida. The group included Harold H. Bailey, who in 1923 suggested a national park in the area south of Lake Okeechobee, and David M. Fairchild, who asked at a meeting on April 14, 1924 what had been done to further this suggestion, and was told that nothing very definite had been accomplished except the establishment of a committee on landscape and park projects.

Dr. Bailey had been with the U. S. Biological Survey (now the U. S. Fish and Wildlife Service); after four years in the Navy Department during and after World War I he came to Florida in the spring of 1920 to collect natural history specimens in the Titusville and Merritt Island area. He then came to Miami Beach to establish a museum and park as an educational project for the Carl G. Fisher organization, which was engaged in the development of Miami Beach.

The Florida Society of Natural History grew out of Bailey's interest in natural history, which was shared by many other local persons. Dr. Bailey credits his father, H. B. Bailey, with suggesting to the newly organized group that a national park should be established in South Florida. In the introduction to his book, *The Birds of Florida*, published in 1924, Harold H. Bailey suggested that an area for birds should be set aside as a state or national park.

Here Ernest F. Coe entered the picture, took up the cause of the Park, and "ran away" with it. Coe came to Miami in 1925 and purchased a home from Hugh M. Matheson in Coconut Grove. Matheson introduced Coe to Bailey as a prospective society member. Coe found himself on the park projects committee, but he apparently went farther and faster than his associates wished to proceed. Coe then sponsored a new organization committed to the single objective of securing a "Tropical Everglades National Park," while the older society turned its attention to having the area first made a wildlife sanctuary to be administered by the U. S. Fish and Wildlife Service as a preliminary to its establishment as a national park.

Coe's new organization, the Tropical Everglades National Park Association, was formed on December 12, 1928 with Dr. Fairchild as president and Coe as executive secretary. There-

Ernest F. Coe, "Father of Everglades National Park," visiting Charles S. "Ted" Smallwood (seated) *at the Smallwood store at Chokoloskee*

after, with little money with which to work (for the national depression hit the country), Coe worked ardently and fervently for the creation of the park. He buttonholed potential supporters, begged financial and moral support, made speeches far and wide, and established contact with every local and national organization that might support his cause.

In June, 1933 Coe induced Jack Ozanne and the Rigby brothers, William and Thomas, to make a much-publicized trip through the Everglades. The three friends had a hunting camp ten miles north of Monroe Station on the Tamiami Trail and knew their way about in the woods. They set out on foot from Royal Palm Hammock on Paradise Key and walked fifteen miles due west, from which point they turned north to the Trail at about Forty Mile Bend where an oil derrick served as a landmark. They spent five days on the trip. High water had reduced the mosquito menace, and on only one night did they fail to find dry ground on which to sleep. Nearly thirty years later Ozanne recalled that the platform of myrtle bushes they piled up on which they went to sleep that night gradually sank into the water. They saw scattered birds and deer, one panther, and four snakes. To the friends it was a lark, but Coe made the most of the venture to promote the project, meeting them with photographers and newspapermen when they emerged from the woods.

In 1929 the Florida legislature approved the formation of a Tropical Everglades National Park Commission of twelve members to be appointed for four-year terms. Coe became executive chairman of the commission, which had power to acquire land by purchase, gift, bequest, or condemnation. Apparently it was to raise its own funds.

On March 1, 1929 the United States Congress authorized an investigation of a specified area in South Florida, requesting a report on its desirability and practicality for a national park. Between February 11 and 17, 1930, the National Park Association, made up of National Park Service personnel and experts from the fields of natural science and conservation, visited the area to collect data. They traveled around, into, and over the Everglades by auto, boat, and the Goodyear blimp, which is wintered in Miami and had been procured for the occasion. This visit produced one of the best descriptive analyses of the region yet published anywhere. The committee's report was submitted May 1, 1931 to Secretary of the Interior Ray Lyman Wilbur, who approved it and passed it along to Congress when it met in December, 1931.

C. Ray Vinten, of the Everglades Park Service, who handled all matters regarding the park in the preliminary stages before it had its own personnel and organization, began to trace each new proposal for boundaries on a map, each identified by a different color. This, appropriately enough, became known as the "rainbow map."

Congressional action was slow. The U.S. Senate three times in as many years passed a park bill dubbed the "Alligator and Snake Swamp Bill" by Republican opponents. On May 14, 1934 the House passed a park bill that insured that nothing would be done immediately by tacking on a provision that no money be appropriated to purchase land for the proposed park for five years. On May 25 the Senate concurred, and on May 31, 1934 President Franklin D. Roosevelt signed the measure.

The area that Congress approved in 1934 had boundaries that extended some fifteen miles above the Tamiami Trail for several miles east to west, and included all of Key Largo and a part of the Florida Reef on the ocean side of the Florida Keys, a total of slightly more than two million acres. However ideal this might have been for park purposes, it was impractical to take that much land out of private use. After a series of boundary adjustments, the area finally established in 1958 was composed of approximately 1,406,000 acres of land and water.

Ernest F. Coe was the leading spokesman for those who wished to see the maximum boundaries included in the park. In fact, his strong insistence upon the larger area began to cause the whole idea, for a while, to lose support. Finally, an eighteen-acre area of Florida Bay on the western side of Key Largo was included to provide a base from which Park waters could be entered from that edge and to protect rookeries on isolated keys in the region. None of the Florida Reef was included.

The depression had spelled the doom for any immediate action. Governor Fred Cone in 1938 appointed G. O. Palmer to succeed Coe, but did not renew appointments of commissioners; there were none until April, 1946 when the body was reactivated to push forward the work of establishing the park. Meanwhile World War II had interrupted all activities for four years.

It is interesting to speculate how much more easily land might have been acquired in the 1930's for a much larger park at a smaller cost and less public opposition than was possible when officials got around to such matters again, for Florida went immediately into a new land boom after World War II and it was more difficult than ever to acquire the necessary land.

In 1944 Florida's Governor-elect Millard F. Caldwell and Governor Spessard L. Holland met with Director Newton B. Drury of the National Park Service to cut the proposed area in order to eliminate over four thousand ownerships of private lands on the periphery of the area and simplify the process of getting the project underway again. At the same time they agreed to turn over to the federal government some 385,693 acres of land and 461,482 acres of water for wildlife conservation; these state properties were to be transferred to the national park when it came into existence. On December 5, 1944, Congress approved.

In 1945 Holland went to the U.S. Senate where he continued to give strong support to the park project, as did Governor Caldwell. In 1946 the governor reactivated the Everglades National Park Commission, and the legislature which authorized it raised the number of commissioners to twenty five. It also provided for a managing director, and appropriated $12,500 for expenses. August Burghard of Fort Lauderdale became the chairman and John D. Pennekamp of the *Miami Herald* was named chairman of the legislative committee. The *Herald* had long supported the park project, as had the *Miami News*, but now Pennekamp made more use than ever of his paper to promote the cause and castigate its enemies.

The need to protect wildlife in the area was so urgent that on October 23, 1946 the Florida Game and Fresh Water Fish Commission and the State Conservation Board commissioned Daniel B. Beard of the U.S. Fish and Wildlife Service and five deputies to make arrests in the future Everglades National Park for violation of state conservation laws. This was a holding operation until the National Park Service would take over the following year and when Beard would also become the first superintendent of the new national park. In addition to its commitment to give its own considerable land holdings in the area, on April 24, 1947 the Florida legislature provided two million dollars to acquire privately-owned lands for the forthcoming Park.

The dedication of Everglades National Park took place at the town of Everglades on Saturday, December 6, 1947. Secretary of the Interior James A. Krug participated and President Harry S. Truman was the principal speaker. Although the town of Everglades was not named as the Park's western gateway until later, the name "Everglades" must have counted heavily in favor of the choice of that site for the ceremonies. After a fish fry there, an afternoon ceremony was also held at Florida City to acknowledge it as the eastern gateway and the only entrance by road into the Park.

When Coe, by common consent recognized as the "Father of Everglades National Park," was hospitalized by his last illness, a Declaration of Taking vesting title to all lands within an area of 1,288,500 acres was approved by the District Court. Thereafter it was possible to go ahead with negotiations and condemnation proceedings to acquire the private lands in the area set aside for the park. This information was conveyed to Coe before his death on January 1, 1951 and was the final realization that the goal for which he had labored so long, so earnestly, and so well had been won.

Some years later Coe's hope that at least part of the Florida Reef would become a park was realized by a combination of federal, state, and private interests. In 1957 President Dwight D. Eisenhower and Florida Governor LeRoy Collins signed papers to set aside a portion of the reef, partly in federal and partly in state waters, to be named the John D. Pennekamp Coral Reef State Park. The problem of providing a land base to administer the park and provide easy access to it was solved by three generous gifts of land. A Miami Beach family who asked to remain anonymous made a gift of 72 acres on the waterfront on Key Largo, and Herbert Shaw gave a fifty foot road right-of-way through his land from the highway to the waterfront property. In the spring of 1963 the same family that made the initial gift provided slightly more than two thousand additional acres of valuable oceanfront land. Finally, in 1967, 27,000 acres of submerged land between the park and its land base were dedicated to the park by the state, connecting it into a single unit of more than 77,000 acres. The only underwater state park in the continental United States, it preserves the sole living coral reef formation in North America.

The largest single donation of private lands for the Park itself was made by the family of Barron G. Collier who acquired some 75 per cent of the land in present day Collier County, which was created in 1923 and named for him. They gave some 32,000 acres, lying east and west of the town of Everglades, that included important parts of the Ten Thousand Islands and the mangrove coast. Everglades City (to distinguish it from the Everglades) is no longer the county seat of Collier County, but will have increasing importance as the western entrance to the Park. A marina on the edge of Chokoloskee Bay, a ranger station, and Park-sponsored boat tours and boatacades were significant early developments there.

Elkhorn Coral at a depth of 25 feet

On the eastern side of the Park an area of some thirty thousand acres known as the "Hole in the Doughnut," originally included in the official boundaries, presents some problems. The owners insisted that their farm lands were too valuable to be taken into the Park, and they received an informal agreement by the land acquisitions authorities that their land would not be condemned for Park use as long as it was used exclusively for agricultural purposes. Farming operations have not been notably successful, but the Federal Farm and Home Administration complicated the situation by lending $400,000 for the development of much of the area for home sites. It became necessary to foreclose the mortgage when the project failed because, the owners said, of the threat of condemnation proceedings to include the area in the Park. Senator Holland urged Congress to provide funds to acquire the land to straighten out the Park's eastern boundary, to simplify the work of patroling the Park, and to restore natural conditions there and in the areas adjacent to it, but at the time of publication of this volume in 1968 its future is still uncertain.

The southern Everglades and related areas remain lands of mystery only to the uninitiated and the unwary who venture there. Main channels are marked, and excellent. Government Coast and Geodetic Survey maps give accurate data for those who choose to use them. Careless navigators may find themselves lost in the maze of islands and channels, however. An example of this occurred even to an official inspection party in the early 1950's. Setting out to view properties along the Gulf coast north and south of Ponce de Leon Bay, they traveled in four cabin cruisers from the old Coot Bay Ranger Station through Joe River and Whitewater Bay and out the mouth of the Shark River to the Gulf of Mexico. They spent all day and it was late when the return trip started. All of the boats had experienced guides so they returned independently. The slowest boat carrying most of the officials appraising the property became hopelessly lost in the overcast night and the maze of mangroves. Even though all the boats had walkie-talkies for short-range communication, the party was not located by searchers until midnight.

Much of the same lure that pioneers found remains for the perceptive Park visitor to experience. Risks endured by early visitors are gone, and going into the Park is no longer high adventure. But it can be richly rewarding. Now twenty years after its dedication more and more people are discovering its beauty and charm and, as anticipated by its early sponsors, more than a million visitors find their way to Everglades National Park each year.

This is not to suggest that all of the Park's problems of creating and maintaining a museum piece of the southern Everglades with its wealth of plants and animals are solved. Alligator poachers and others who occasionally hunt and fish in the area illegally are now at a mere nuisance level. Objections to the Park's boundaries have largely subsided. The urgent problem is the assurance of enough fresh water to retain for the Park the natural state that it was meant to preserve. The Park once received water that fell as far north as the Kissimmee River valley and Lake Okeechobee, but it is now possible that it will be reduced to dependence upon the water that falls on it.

The water supply is dependent upon policy regarding the use of water impounded in Reservoir Three north of the Tamiami Trail across the northern boundary of the Park. This reservoir is part of the gigantic water control program for the Central and Southern Florida Flood Control District, which includes all of the Florida Everglades northward to Lake Okeechobee. If there is sufficient volume to release large amounts into the Park in times of need, this may be the assurance needed to keep alive much of the plant and animal life associated with it. There are, however, insistent demands that the water be reserved first for the increasing human needs of the rapidly growing population on Florida's lower east coast. At this writing in 1967 the Park has been promised an equitable share of the water, but how this is to be accomplished is not yet determined.

Park officials are also greatly concerned about the effects of drainage and development on the land between the Park area and the Atlantic Ocean. For example, a new barge canal known as C-111, also designed to provide drainage in high water, will almost surely lower the water table under the eastern part of the Park and let in salt water during periods of drought such as were experienced in the springs of 1966 and 1967, thereby altering the ecology of a fresh water area.

People in Florida as elsewhere in the nation will be forced again and again to make far-reaching decisions between conflicting interests and values.

BIBLIOGRAPHY

Anonymous. "Notes on the Passage Across the Everglades," *Tequesta*, XX (1960), pp. 57–65.

Audubon, John James. "Three Florida Episodes," *Tequesta*, V (1945), pp. 52–68. (From *The Life of John James Audubon the Naturalist*, ed. by his widow. New York: G. P. Putnam's Sons, 1879.)

Bailey, Harold Harris. *The Birds of Florida*. Baltimore: privately pub., 1925.

Barbour, Thomas. *That Vanishing Eden, A Naturalist's Florida*. Boston: Little, Brown, 1944.

Bartram, William. *The Travels of William Bartram*. Facsimile Library ed., Mark Doren, ed. New York: Dover, 1940.

Brookfield, Charles M. and Oliver Griswold. *They All Called It Tropical*. Miami: Data Press, 5th ed., 1957.

Canova, Andrew P. *Life and Adventures in South Florida*. Tampa: Tribune Printing Co., 1904.

Carter, Clarence E., comp. and ed. *The Territorial Papers of the United States*. XXII (1821–1824), 1957; XXIII (1824–1828), 1958; XXIV (1828–1832), 1959; XXV (1834–1839), 1960; XXVI (The Territory of Florida, 1839–1845), 1962. Washington: Government Printing Office.

Chapman, Frank M. *Camp and Cruises of An Ornithologist*. New York: Appleton and Co., 1908.

Cooke, C. Wythe. "Scenery of Florida Interpreted by a Geologist," *Geological Bul. No. 17*. Tallahassee: Fla. State Dept. of Conservation, 1939.

Covington, James W., ed. "Exploring the Ten Thousand Islands in 1838," *Tequesta*, XVIII (1958), pp. 7–13.

Craighead, F. C. and V. C. Gilbert. "The Effect of Hurricane Donna on the Vegetation of South Florida," *Quarterly Journal of the Fla. Academy of Sciences*, 25:1 (March, 1962), pp. 1–28.

Cushing, Frank Hamilton. "Exploration of Ancient Key Dwellers' Remains on the Gulf Coast of Florida," *Proceedings of the American Philosophical Society*, Vol. 35 (1897), pp. 329–448.

Davis, John H., Jr. "The Natural Features of Southern Florida, Especially the Vegetation of the Everglades," *Geological Bul. No. 25*. Tallahassee: Dept. of Conservation, 1943.

Dimock, Anthony W. *Florida Enchantments*. New York: Stokes (rev. ed.), 1926.

Doubleday, Russell. *A Year in a Yawl; From the Log of Captain Ransom*. New York, 1901.

Douglas, Marjory Stoneman. *The Everglades: River of Grass.* New York: Rinehart & Co., 1947.

Fontaneda, Hernando d' Escalante. *Memoir of D°. d'Escalante Fontaneda Respecting Florida* (Spain, ca. 1474). Tr. by Buckingham Smith, Washington, 1854. Reprinted with revisions, David O. True. ed. Miami: Univ. of Miami and Hist. Assn. of Southern Fla., 1944.

Gilpin, Mrs. John R. "Diary of a West Coast Sailing Expedition, 1885," *Tequesta,* VII (1947), pp. 44–64.

Goggin, John M. "Archaeological Investigations on the Upper Florida Keys," *Tequesta,* No. 4 (1944), pp. 13–35.

Griswold, Oliver. *The Florida Keys and the Coral Reef.* Miami: Graywood Press, 1965.

Hammond, E. A. "Doctor Strobel Reports on Southeast Florida, 1836," *Tequesta,* XXI (1961), pp. 65–75.

Hanna, A. J. *Flight Into Oblivion.* New York: Barnes and Noble, 1938.

Harper, Roland M. "Natural Resources of Southern Florida," *18th Annual Report.* Tallahassee: Fla. State Geological Survey, 1927.

Holder, Charles Frederick. *Along the Florida Reef.* New York, 1892.

Howell, Arthur H. *Florida Bird Life.* New York: Coward McCann, 1932.

Hrdlicka, Ales. *The Anthropology of Florida.* Deland, Fla.: Fla. Hist. Publ. No. 1, 1922.

Job, Herbert K. *Wild Wings.* Boston: Houghton Mifflin Co., 1905.

McNicoll, Robert E. "The Caloosa Village Tequesta: A Miami of the Sixteenth Century," *Tequesta,* No. 1 (1941), pp. 11–20.

MacCauley, Clay. *Personal Characteristics of Florida Seminoles.* Washington: Bur. of Amer. Ethnology, Smithsonian Misc. Col., Vol. 25, 1883.

Manuey, Albert. "The Gibraltar of the Gulf of Mexico," *Florida Historical Quarterly,* XXI, pp. 303–331.

Moore, Clarence B. "Certain Antiquities of the Florida West Coast," *Journal of the Academy of Natural Sciences of Philadelphia,* Vol. II (1900), pp. 349–394.

Nash, Roy. *Survey of the Seminole Indians of Florida.* Washington: Senate Document No. 314 (71st Congress, 3rd Session), 1931.

Neill, Wilfred T. *Florida's Seminole Indians.* St. Petersburg: Great Outdoors Publishing Co., 1956.

Pearse, Eleanor H. D. *Florida's Vanishing Era.* Privately printed, 1954.

Pierce, Charles W. "The Cruise of the Bonton," *Tequesta,* XXII (1962), pp. 3–63.

Robertson, William B., Jr. *Everglades, The Park Story.* Coral Gables: Univ. of Miami Press, 1959.

Robertson, William B., Jr. "Ornithology of 'The Cruise of the Bonton'," *Tequesta,* XXII (1962), pp. 65–77.

Robertson, William B., Jr. "The Terns of the Dry Tortugas," *Bul. of the Fla. State Museum,* Vol. 8, No. 1, 1964.

Romans, Bernard. A *Concise Natural History of East and West Florida.*

A Facsimile Reproduction of the 1775 Edition, Rembert W. Patrick, ed. Gainesville: Univ. of Fla. Press, 1962.

Safford, W. E. "Natural History of Paradise Key and the Nearby Everglades of Florida," *Smithsonian Report for 1917.* Washington: Smithsonian Inst. Publ. No. 2508, pp. 377–434, 1919.

Sears, William H. "The Turner River Site, Collier County, Florida," *Florida Anthropologist,* IX (June, 1956), pp. 47–60.

Simpson, Charles Torrey. *In Lower Florida Wilds.* New York, 1920.

Small, John Kunkel. *Eden to Sahara.* Lancaster, Pa.: Science Press, 1919.

Sturtevant, William C. "Chakaika and the 'Spanish Indians'," *Tequesta,* XIII (1953), pp. 35–74.

Tebeau, Charlton W. *Chokoloskee Bay Country.* Coral Gables: Univ. of Miami Press, 1955.

Tebeau, Charlton W. *Florida's Last Frontier.* Coral Gables: Univ. of Miami Press, rev. ed. 1966.

Will, Lawrence E. *Dredgeman of Cape Sable.* St. Petersburg: Great Outdoors Publishing Co., 1966.

Williams, John Lee. *The Territory of Florida.* New York: Goodrich, 1837.

Willoughby, Hugh L. *Across the Everglades: A Canoe Journey of Exploration.* Philadelphia: Lippincott, 1898.

Wintringham, Mary K., ed. "North to South Through the Glades in 1885," *Tequesta,* XXIII (1963), pp. 33–59; XXIV (1964), pp. 59–93.

INDEX